# The Offering

## How to Emerge from Shattered Faith

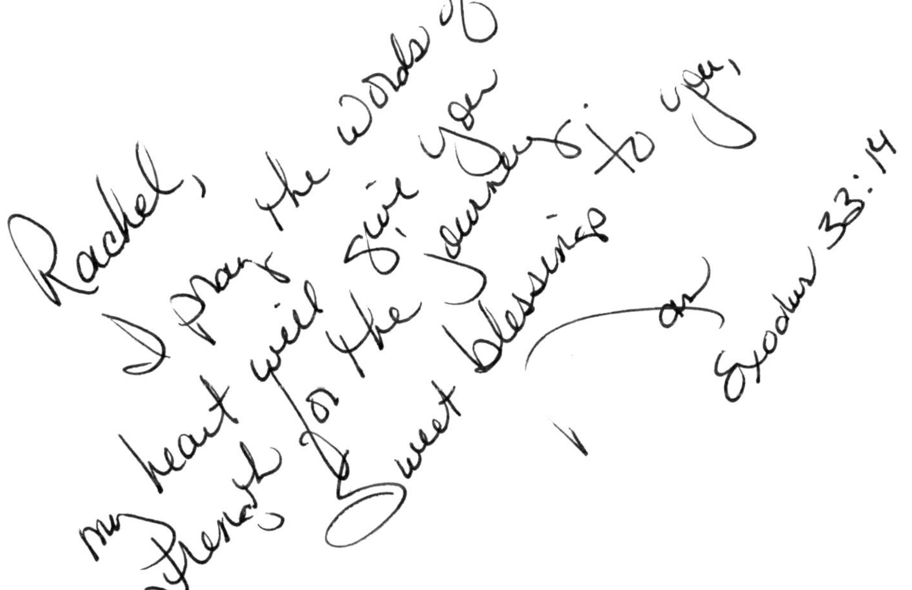

# Endorsements

As someone who has experienced the heart-wrenching pain of having their faith shattered, I cannot recommend *The Offering: How to Emerge from Shattered Faith* enough. This powerful and insightful book offers a road map for anyone struggling to emerge from the darkness of doubt and despair. With honesty and vulnerability, the author shares her own journey and offers practical wisdom and encouragement for others who are navigating the same difficult terrain.

What I appreciate most about *The Offering* is it doesn't offer simplistic answers or platitudes. Instead, the book acknowledges the complexity and depth of the struggle and offers a compassionate and hopeful perspective on what it means to walk through the valley of the shadow of doubt.

Whether you are in the midst of a crisis of faith or simply seeking to deepen your spiritual journey, *The Offering* is a must-read. It will challenge and inspire you, and ultimately, leave you with a deeper sense of hope and faith amid life's most difficult challenges.
—**Rev. David Blackburn**, director of missions Ashe Baptist Association

Occasionally, a book resonates so deeply we feel we could have written the very words contained within. *The Offering: How to Emerge from Shattered Faith* is one of

those books for me. Pain in its various forms is inevitable: physical, emotional, relational, financial, spiritual, and even secondary pain, yet we get to choose how we will respond. Will we allow it to crush us, push God away, and retreat, or will our pain be a catalyst that causes us to lean in and learn all he has to teach us through our sacrificed ashes of pain upon his altar? Nan vulnerably shares her own story of devastating pain and loss and takes readers by the hand so they know they aren't alone. Take Nan's hand in one of yours and this book in the other. You'll be forever changed.
—**Dr. Michelle Bengtson**, author of the award-winning book *Breaking Anxiety's Grip: How to Reclaim the Peace God Promises* and host of *Your Hope Filled Perspective* podcast.

Nan shares openly and honestly from the depth of her pain what it means to truly surrender to the God who loves and cares for us. Her insight with steps to move forward after heartbreak is transformational to anyone's walk with Christ.
—**Sharon Dodds**, *handsofhope.com* (ministry for widows)

The beauty of brokenness must be perceived before the transformation from ashes can be made an offering. Nan has discovered how shattered expectations bring clarity, forging worship during affliction. There is the life and the Lifegiver walking with us through the valley of the shadow where self-life dies. The very indwelling Life of Christ causes us to desire the offer only he can grow to the glory of his name. Read and be blessed!
—**Paul**, a fellow worshipper.

If suffering has made you question your once rock-solid faith, this book is for you. With biblical accuracy, profound vulnerability, and extraordinary wisdom, Nan Jones will help you discover beauty among the ashes. *The Offering* is an exquisitely written book that gently leads the reader to

a place of clinging once again to the unparalleled love of God. You'll want to purchase extra copies to give away.
—**Carol Kent**, founder and executive director of Speak Up Ministries; speaker and author of *When I Lay My Isaac Down* (NavPress)

It might seem an odd pairing to bring God's Grin Gal to the subjects found in *The Offering* by Nan Jones. But it's just the right fit because learning how to emerge from shattered faith is the only way we can find grace that leads to authentic grins of face and heart. The book begins with Nan's personal journey and gives practical and biblical takeaways to the reader. My favorite section is the journal portion of the book, with space to process the stages of lament, offering, and restoration. Nan's gritty prayers get to the deep. Not many faith-based books address the importance of lament to regain hope. We all deal with pain and suffering. Instead of allowing it to crush us, we can come to God while yet struggling and find his presence for our peace. Nan's book leads us to that hope.
—**Kathy Carlton Willis**, God's Grin Gal. Speaker and author of multiple books, including *Your Life on Hold: Don't Hate the Wait*. www.kathycarltonwillis.com

*The Offering: How to Emerge from Shattered Faith* is Nan Jones's wheelhouse. Filled with teaching and thought-provoking chapters, she guides us on how to pull free from a shattered faith. A nice must-have for every nightstand, you'll find amazing insights filled with love and inspiration.
—**Cindy K. Sproles**, author of *Meet Me Where I Am, Lord* and *This is Where It Ends*

# The Offering

## How to Emerge from Shattered Faith

NAN JONES

A Christian Company
ElkLakePublishingInc.com

# Copyright Notice

*The Offering: How to Emerge from Shattered Faith*



Cover and Interior Design: Derinda Babcock, Deb Haggerty
Editor(s): Kristin Cooney, Judy Hagey, Deb Haggerty

PUBLISHED BY: Elk Lake Publishing, Inc., 35 Dogwood Drive, Plymouth, MA 02360, 2023

---

**Library Cataloging Data**

Names: Jones, Nan (Nan Jones)

*The Offering: How to Emerge from Shattered Faith* / Nan Jones

196 p. 23cm × 15cm (9in × 6 in.)

ISBN-13: 978-1-64949-988-2 (paperback) | 978-1-64949-989-9 (trade hardcover) | 978-1-64949-990-5 (trade paperback) | 978-1-64949-991-2 (e-book)

Restoring faith; Emotional healing; Finding God again; Where is God when it hurts; Suffering; Brokenness; Grief counseling resources

Library of Congress Control Number: 2023943882 Nonfiction

*The Offering* is dedicated to those whose tears have soaked the feet of Jesus as you reached desperately for the hem of His garment ... and then gave up. Blinded by pain, your heart turned cold. I know. I've been there. I kept your hearts before me as I wrote, listened, and prayed, "Lord, use my story to help these, my friends." My prayers for you continue today.

May your heart receive healing, and your faith emerge from the shattered places.

# Table of Contents

# Acknowledgments

I'm so thankful the Lord entrusted me with the message of *The Offering*. I didn't think I could survive the pain, but I did—only because of His grace, His longsuffering, and His unfailing love. And as a result, I can now comfort you, my reader, with the comfort I have received. I'm so grateful.

I want to acknowledge my precious husband, David. Although in the beginning, he was the villain, he has since become my treasured reward in this redemption story. Dementia is taking its toll, but his spirit remains strong. I cherish his prayers. Although simple and childlike now, his prayers are where heaven meets earth.

My children, Dave Jr., Matthew, and Nancy are heaven-sent. They and their spouses, Denise, Nina, and Andy, have held my hands, dried my tears, and offered unselfish support in the care of their dad. This manuscript reached completion because of their love.

My best friend, Marcie Bridges, has been instrumental in keeping my hand on the plow, providing an extra set of eyes and helping me find laughter on the hardest of days. Thank you, Marcie girl.

And I would be remiss if I didn't mention the Alabaster Girls, my online prayer and Bible study fellowship, many of whom belong to my prayer team for which I am so thankful. Ladies, you are a precious gift from the Father.

Your encouragement and prayer support undergird me in magnificent ways and infuse me with the strength of Jesus. I am blessed by walking this journey of faith with you.

I also want to thank Deb Haggerty of Elk Lake Publishing, Inc. for believing in this message created to meet a felt need among the body of Christ. I appreciate her godly leadership of ELPI. I appreciate my editor, Kristin Cooney, whose skill and beautiful heart made *The Offering* shine for the glory of God, and Derinda Babcock who helped me fine-tune a cover design that would call out to you, my reader, who is searching for hope among the shattered pieces of her life. Thank you, Derinda, for your kindness with me.

But as it is written:

"Eye has not seen, nor ear heard,
Nor have entered into the heart of man
The things which God has prepared for
those who love Him." (1 Corinthians 2:9)

I am blessed.

*Bring Me your sorrow, and watch for the sunrise of the resurrection. Yes, truly there comes always a resurrection—a morning when hope is reborn and life*
*finds new beginning. Wait for it as tulip bulbs anticipate the spring.*
*The rarest blooms are enhanced by the coldness of winter. The snow plays her part in producing spring's pageant. But when the blossoms*
*break through, we do not then turn back to thoughts of winter, but instead, we look ahead to the*
*full joys of the coming summer.*
*So, you must do also. Your God is your maker.*
*He is your defender. And He is mighty to save.*
*Yes, He is not only mighty to save from sin, but He is mighty to save from despair, from sorrow,*
*from disappointment,*
*from regret, from remorse, from self-castigation, and from the hot, blinding tears of rebellion against fateful circumstances. He can save you from yourself, and He loves you when you find it hard*
*to love yourself.*

*Let His peace flow in you like a river, carrying away*
*all the poison of painful memories, and*
*bringing to you a fresh, clear stream of pure life*
*and restoring thoughts.*

—Frances J. Roberts,
*Come Away My Beloved*[1]

# A Personal Note from Nan

Seasons of pain and difficulty may come to each of us at any given time. We live in a fallen world where bad things happen to good people. Brokenness abounds. Injustice wreaks havoc. Sorrow, anger, bitterness, or depression can consume us like a flash flood roaring through a mountain canyon without notice.

It happens.

Our lives are forever changed in a moment.

Do we hold God accountable? Usually. And in these angered accusations hurled at the One who loves us, do we build our walls of separation one dreadful stone at a time, attempting to keep Him out? Yes. Unfortunately. After all, the Lord let us down, didn't He? *Where were His promises to preserve and keep me? Why didn't He protect me from this work of the enemy? How can this devastation be an expression of love?*

The components of each story may look different, but I assure you the heart condition is the same. Divorce weaves bitterness into our souls. The death of a child creates unfathomable sorrow, ripping our hearts to shreds and leaving us drowning in our tears. The suicide of a loved one, relentless suffering from cancer, heartache from a prodigal child ... these all look the same through our shattered rose-colored glasses—the glasses that once embraced our faith.

And the result is the same: We begin to question the faithfulness of God. Where is He? Why did He allow this to happen to me? Why would He abandon me in my most desperate need?

I assure you of this: You are not alone. Many have walked this broken road.

I found Jesus at the end of my road—arms wide open waiting for me with healing and restoration in His hands. He opened my eyes to see Him, awakened my heart to understand His great love.

And as He taught me to lay my pain on His altar of mercy and grace—to offer my broken heart as a sacrifice to Him—beauty rose from the sacred ashes.

I can't wait to help you do the same. Our circumstances may vary, but I assure you the pain is the same, the brokenness is the same. The devastation of shattered faith that left my spirit gasping for breath is the *same* devastation you are experiencing now.

But there is a way to overcome and be restored.

That way is learning *The Offering*.

# Chapter One—How Long, O God, Will You Forget Me?

> We need never shout across the spaces to an absent God. He is nearer than our own soul, closer than our most secret thoughts.
>
> —Tozer

A secret rendezvous disclosed through a careless text cursed my world. I struggled to breathe as the very breath was sucked out of me—a punch in the gut would have been more merciful than this. As the sun set across our mountain ridge, so the darkness fell upon my marriage of thirty-one years, the glory of the painted sky mocking the black shroud descending on my soul.

We had been a team—David and I. A force to be reckoned with within the walls of ministry. Together we fought in the trenches for the sake of righteousness. We endured fierce battles when religious leaders felt their grasp on control slipping away. We witnessed lives change. Hearts of stone melt.

And our love grew.

But now the marriage others envied and desired, or so we were told, lay shattered at my feet, shaken to its core, strangled by the destructive tentacles of adultery.

My knees buckled, hurling me to the floor. Sobs rumbled through my heart and escaped through my lips—groans too deep for words. My body quaked in disbelief. I remember a scream—a scream of primal origin—but the remaining moments fade into a foggy blur like a cloudy mist that hovers and shrouds our regal mountaintops.

Yet this I know and remember well: My heart lay shattered beneath my bent knees.

How did we get to this place of horror? Yes, I know the unthinkable act of adultery happens all the time in marriages everywhere. But our marriage was different. Really. Not just rhetorically but really. Our marriage was not your average American marriage. We had not only made a covenant with each other—we had made a covenant with God. His anointing had been upon us.

We had cherished one another for thirty-one years, and now ...

Thirty-one years. I cannot begin to describe the crushing emotional pain I was suffering. My faith lay shattered at my feet as I desperately clung to the cross. As days turned into weeks, and weeks turned into months, I began to understand something: God had been preparing me to face a trial of this magnitude for many years—not with my marriage, per se, for it had been strong and sure. But I now know He used painful life events to prepare me for this spiritual battle that would seek to devour me. Over the course of my lifetime, the Lord had been teaching me of His faithfulness, His steadfast love. These lessons were stepping stones to a lifeline I didn't know I would need until the unthinkable happened.

You recognize this kind of battle, or perhaps you wouldn't be reading this book.

Charles Spurgeon, an esteemed preacher from the late 1800s, once reportedly said, "Groans that words cannot express are often prayers that God cannot refuse." The kind of pain you and I have experienced—different circumstances, same intensity—is surely composed of groans that only a heavenly Father could recognize as desperate prayer.

My groans began in earnest in 2003 with the suicide of my brother. I remember that day so well.

Shadows cast from the moonlight obscured the dresser top as I fumbled in the dark for my phone.

"Nan." It was Daddy. He paused. Hesitant. "Nan, Don is gone. His body was found at his home today. He's dead, sweetheart."

I fell against the wall and slid to the cold, hard floor. I stammered, struggling to breathe and grasp the horrifying news.

The thing I feared most of all had come to pass: My brother had taken his life.

I thought of Don's gentle brown eyes that glimmered with kindness—a kindness that masked a deep depression. He was such a good man. I couldn't believe he was gone. Don had used alcohol for years to numb the pain of childhood traumas, but that pain had finally proved too great to overcome. His depression became the victor in the battle for his life.

Survivors of a loved one's suicide often wallow in guilt and remorse and regret. In most cases these emotions are irrational, but the survivors feel them, nevertheless. Memories haunted me. Regrets aimed their torments straight at my heart as my imagination carried me to the moment of Don's death. How alone he must have felt. How desperate he must have been. My heart shattered for my precious brother.

I flung angry accusations at the Lord. Why had He not delivered Don from the talons of depression? Why didn't God send someone to stop him? Why, oh why, did this have to happen? God, in His tenderness, loved me through my tantrum. I could sense His nearness, His comfort.

But I couldn't pray. Not really. Not then.

All I could do was moan and slip into a silent scream.

Six weeks later, my daddy was diagnosed with leukemia. Seven months after the diagnosis, he died. In my agonized state, deep called to deep. Like whitewater rapids, the depth of my grief left me plummeting toward another unbearable loss, crushing me in its wake. Sorrow heaped upon sorrow. My heart ripped in two. The brokenness of my spirit began to engulf me.

And it didn't stop there.

The next few months brought the death of a close friend from ovarian cancer—the friend I had prayed for and believed for her healing. Not long after her death, my husband and I were asked to leave the church we had pastored for several years. The power players of the church won the battle and voted us out. The congregants were like family to us. We had been with them through their greatest joys and held them through their darkest moments. In one quick business meeting, our church family was jerked from our lives.

*God, where are You?* A numbness of spirit settled in. I spiraled down into a dark and lonely place—a place I detested, but a place I did not have the strength to escape. The darkness frightened me. I had not known anguish this great before—this deep. It was more than I could endure. I felt abandoned by the Lord I loved.

Have you ever felt this way—abandoned by God? By the One you've trusted and served with your life? It's a dismal place, isn't it? I felt empty. Betrayed. I believed the Lord when He promised to never leave me nor forsake me ... so where was He? Didn't He have the responsibility to protect me from this heartbreak? He is greater than the enemy of this world who wanted to wear me down, tear me up, and stop my witness.

My witness ... just my witness alone should afford me an abundant life complete with joy and peace. Right? Wrong. Joy and peace escaped me. Even though I loved the Lord and served His Church and His people faithfully, now I felt totally abandoned by the One who promised He would always be with me. Yes, abandoned. Where was God when I needed Him the most? What about His promise?

The talons of grief suffocated me. The light within me grew dim as doubts wove their deceptive web. I shuffled through the routines of every day, but something—Someone—was missing.

One evening, I stood at the kitchen sink washing dinner dishes, my thoughts lost in the warm suds swishing between my fingers. I was on cruise control—not thinking, not reacting. Just breathing. Barely. Deep in my spirit, a song began to rise, a familiar hymn buried beneath the contemporary worship songs of today.

My hands stopped. I stood still, cocked my head a little, closed my eyes, and opened my mouth. Out of my lips flowed a lifeline:

> On a hill far away stood an old rugged cross,
> the emblem of suffering and shame.

*Lord? Is that You?*

> [A]nd I love that old cross where the dearest and best
> for a world of lost sinners was slain.

Salty tears tumbled down my cheeks and dripped into the dishwater. My head fell forward as I rested my forearms against the counter. Quietly, I embraced the chorus:

> So I'll cherish the old rugged cross,
> till my trophies, at last, I lay down;
> I will cling to the old rugged cross,
> and exchange it some day for a crown.[1]

I held my face in my hands and slipped to my knees. *Oh Lord, I need You. I need to know You are with me like You promised. My life is engulfed in sorrow. I am so broken. Only You can put me back together again. Only You. But I can't sense You near me. Please help me, Lord. Help me see You. Open my eyes. Open my ears that I might hear You.*

I remained kneeling for a long while. Quiet. Still. Remembering He is God, remembering I am His child and nothing can separate me from His love. I stretched out on the kitchen floor and rested in that moment while His great love washed over me. On that cold floor, the Lord revealed Himself to me, and I knew I wasn't alone—He had never left nor forsaken me. I determined that day to root this truth in me so when the tsunamis of sorrow and anguish washed over me again, I'd stand in the knowledge that I was not alone.

The following thought-provoking words found in the devotional *Streams in the Desert* by L. B. Cowman have ministered greatly to me during my time of seeking to understand the purpose in my sorrow. Perhaps they will speak to your heart also.

> There is a divine mystery in suffering, one that has a strange and supernatural power and has never been completely understood by human reason. No one has ever developed a deep level of spirituality or holiness without experiencing a great deal of suffering. When a person who suffers reaches a point where he can be calm and carefree, inwardly smiling at his own suffering and no longer asking God to be delivered from it, then the suffering has accomplished its blessed ministry, perseverance has "finish[ed] its work" (James 1:4), and the pain of the crucifixion has begun to weave itself into a crown. Oh, my goodness! ... "[T]he Crucifixion has begun to weave itself ...
>
> It is in this experience of complete suffering that the Holy Spirit works many miraculous things deep within our

> soul. In this condition, our entire being lies perfectly still under the hand of God; every power and ability of the mind, will, and heart are at last submissive; a quietness of eternity settles into the entire soul; and finally, the mouth becomes quiet, having only a few words to say, and stops crying out the words Christ quoted on the cross: "My God, my God, why have you forsaken me?" (Psalm 22:1).[2]

Did you catch the phrase "then the suffering has accomplished its blessed ministry, perseverance has 'finish[ed] its work' (James 1:4), and the pain of the crucifixion has begun to weave itself into a crown"? Oh, my goodness! ... "[T]he Crucifixion has begun to weave itself into a crown." I love the imagery these words create. Our suffering has an eternal purpose. We gain insight into the mysteries of Christ. A deep understanding of the essence of God grows and develops in our spirit. And the best gain of all? "A quietness of eternity settles into the entire soul," complete rest in the knowledge and appreciation of God's sovereignty.

But this doesn't negate the pain of sorrow, suffering, anguish ... despair.

What I'm learning is the sweetness amid the bitterness is the Lord Himself, but until we learn to open our eyes to see Him in our midst, the bitterness continues to permeate our spirit and destroy us. Psalm 34:18 tells us the Lord is drawn to the brokenhearted. But do we believe it? Maybe in our mind, but this needs to become heart knowledge. The realization that the God of the universe is with me when I'm hurting—because He wants to be—becomes an amazing comfort.

But the realization of His presence only comes when we learn to see beyond the veil that separates the physical realm from the spiritual. When everything in our soul cries out in despair and everything reasonable tells us that certainly, God is nowhere to be found—He has abandoned us—and yet, He gently lifts our chin and whispers, *Child, open your eyes to see Me. I am here* ... well, there is absolutely nothing like it. No comfort can compare. It is a miracle of miracles. The realization of His presence is a resting place for a troubled mind.

When we seek to find the Lord in our struggles, we can learn from the psalmist David. In Psalm 10, David is in distress because he sees the wicked prospering. His mounting frustration leads him to ask God for answers. I love David's authentic relationship with the Lord. It was not cloaked in piety or self-righteousness. It was, at times, wrought with raw emotion and honest, gut-level questions, because like us, David also wrestled with moments of despair:

> Why do You stand afar off, O LORD?
> Why do You hide in times of trouble?" (Psalm 10:1)

He asked God questions:

> How long, O LORD? Will You forget me
> forever?
> How long will You hide Your face from me?
> How long shall I take counsel in my soul,
> *Having* sorrow in my heart daily?
> How long will my enemy be exalted over me?
> (Psalm 13:1–2)

After pouring out his doubts and fears, David always encouraged himself in the Lord:

> But I have trusted in Your mercy;
> My heart shall rejoice in Your salvation.
> I will sing to the LORD,
> Because He has dealt bountifully with me."
> (Psalm 13:5–6)

He remembered God's faithfulness:

> The Lord also will be a refuge for the oppressed,
> A refuge in times of trouble.
> And those who know Your name will
> put their trust in You;
> For You, Lord, have not forsaken those
> who seek You." (Psalm 9:9–10).

He reminded the Lord of His covenant love for His children (Psalm 105). David remembered who he was in light of who God is (Psalm 8). Perhaps, had David been alive when Jesus walked the earth, he too would have sung "I will cling to the old rugged cross, and exchange it some day for a crown," for it is in the work of the cross that we gain intimate fellowship with the Lord. *He* is our exceedingly great reward (Genesis 15:1). It's because of the cross we can run to the Lord, who is our strong tower when the enemy assails. It's because of the cross we can open our eyes to behold our magnificent God and see beyond the veil.

Beyond the veil. What does that mean? Certainly, as Christians we've been taught that at the moment of Jesus's death, the veil in the temple was torn in two from the top to the bottom, symbolizing we were no longer separated from God and could approach Him individually.

But this is not the veil I'm referring to.

I'm referring to the veil that clouds our vision—the invisible veil that opposes the Scripture teaching us to walk by faith and not by sight (2 Corinthians 5:7). When we choose to walk by *sight* in our times of despair, often God is nowhere to be found. Have you experienced this? I sure have. When our heart is breaking, and our mind can't handle any more stress, our flesh wants to take over and scream, "God, where are You? I can't see You! How do I know You are near?"

Another quote frequently attributed to Charles Spurgeon reads, "God is too good to be unkind. He is too wise to make a mistake. If I cannot trace His hand, I can always trust His heart." But like the psalmist David, first we must believe the Lord is drawn to the brokenhearted. We must believe His love for His child is beyond comprehension. We must *believe* we can always trust His heart.

Even when our circumstances say otherwise.

I live in the mountains of North Carolina. When summer transitions into fall or winter yields to the birth of spring, thick fog is a common occurrence. Warm air and cold air butt up against one another, eclipsing the mountaintops. The mountain ridges stand in a shroud of foggy mist oyster-gray in color. Thick clouds hang low, obliterating the landscape, obscuring the winding roads and mountain ridges. How do I know the mountain ridge is still there when I can't see it? Because I'm familiar with my surroundings. How can I find my way along the winding road where visibility is nearly impossible? I can find my way because I'm familiar with the road. I know the landscape.

Trusting in God's presence is much the same. When we are familiar with Him and His promises, when we spend time learning His character and absorbing His grace, then we can say with full assurance, "My God is with me." Even when my vision is obscured, and I can't trace His hand, I know He is with me because He promised. And in those horrid moments of despair when all seems lost and everything within screams abandonment, know this: God's love is not contingent on our attitude, and the assurance of His presence with us is not contingent on the level of faith we have at that moment. Honestly, I believe when we trust Him enough to have a full-blown tantrum over our perceived disappointment in Him, His mercy and grace go into overdrive to reassure us as His children. In those moments, I believe He is waiting for us to ask Him, "God, where are You?"

Maybe you are asking that question now. Perhaps life has come at you hard, and you can't seem to find the strength ... or the desire ... to go on. Like me, maybe your faith was the one thing in your life that was for sure, something you depended on and sacrificed for. But now with your faith in crisis, you are wondering if God has abandoned you. I encourage you to ask the difficult questions. Find the necessary answers that will help you break the chains binding you.

Isaiah 45:2–3 is fitting for this moment:

I will go before you
And make the crooked places straight;
I will break into pieces the gates of bronze
And cut the bars of iron.
I will give you the treasures of darkness
And hidden riches of secret places,
That you may know that I, the Lord,
Who call *you* by your name,
*Am* the God of Israel.

Are you ready? I know the Father is anxious to help you find the treasures in your darkness and the hidden riches of His secret place reserved especially for His child who is hurting.

May I pray for you?

*Father, in Your infinite wisdom, You prepare a path for our lives, and when that path becomes crooked, You promise to make it straight. You promise to be light in our darkness. You promise to bring refreshing streams to our desert places. Thank You for Your faithfulness to Your children.*

*I ask that You bring healing through the pages of this book as we learn to offer our pain to You as a form of worship. Receive our offering, Lord. Restore the faith the enemy has tried to steal. Open the eyes of my sister so she might see You in the midst of her pain. Help her see beyond the veil that obscures her vision of You and open her ears so she might hear Your sweet whispers of love. Encourage her. Restore to her the joy of her salvation.*

*And above all, I ask that You answer her questions of "Where are You?" when her life crumbles, and her heart breaks in two. Help her emerge from this horribly shattered faith. Thank You for hearing us when we cry out to You. Thank You for loving us with such magnificent love.*

# Chapter Two—Satisfying the Thirst of an Empty Soul

> It is only into the thirst of an empty soul that the streams of living waters flow.
>
> Ever thirsting is the secret of never thirsting.
>
> —Andrew Murray

My heart raced with anxiety. Thoughts piled awkwardly on top of thoughts until they toppled over, pulling me into a downward spiral. I jumped from one task to another, never completing the one before I had my hands dirty in another. It was pointless. I felt pointless. Worthless. Incompetent.

Striving. Reaching.

Never enough. Ever.

Then right in the middle of my pity party, the Spirit of God whispered, *Abide in Me, live within My love. Rest in My secret place beneath the shadow of My wing.*

My response?

*Seriously, God? You want me to stop what I'm doing and sit? I don't think so. I'll never finish if I stop.*

*Nan, you'll never finish if you don't stop. Cease striving. Be still.*

And that's what I did. Finally.

I stepped away from the circus controlling my life, struggling to dismiss the shame of adultery's scandal and the horror of wrestling with a faith shaken to its core. I realized the world would not cease its spinning if I hopped off the gerbil wheel and learned to rest in God. I took time to focus on Him. I took time to find out how to rest in Him—to abide in Him and not in my sorrow. I had thought I could hide in the sorrow, that somehow magically the breaking of my heart and soul and mind couldn't go any further if I didn't address it. Yes, hiding in busyness was much better. Or so it seemed.

But God was showing me a better way.

I began to see the Lord as a *place* of refuge outside myself.

In my quest to understand, the Lord took me to John 15:4: "Abide in Me, and I in you." The Amplified Bible, Classic Edition, reads "Dwell in Me, and I will dwell in you. [Live in Me, and I will live in you.]" For years, I have been drawn to this verse. Long before I began a fervent search for the Lord in my struggles, I pondered this passage. I could see the concept. I could understand, and yet ... my eyes were still veiled to grasp the reality of the Lord's presence.

I could understand how the Lord lives within the believer of Jesus Christ through the indwelling power of the Holy Spirit, but for the life of me, I couldn't comprehend how I lived *in* Him. Surely the presence of the Lord God wasn't limited to containment within my broken, fragile self. If His Spirit in my life could only be found *in* me, then how could I run to Him? How could I rest in Him? How could He be my strong tower, my place of refuge?

Wasn't I keeping God in the proverbial box if I limited His access to myself in terms of only dwelling in me? Filtering the mighty God through my limitations (even if subconsciously) reduced Him to something or Someone I could understand. But He's bigger than that. I couldn't figure it out—not until I began to pray, *Lord, open my eyes to see.*

I began to pray in earnest, *Lord, open my eyes that I might see, open my ears that I might hear Your sweet whispers of love.* Almighty God, in His faithfulness, heard my cry and began to teach me His truths—His mysteries found in Christ. He taught me to take Him out of the box in which I unknowingly contained His majesty and power. To sense His presence in the mighty wind rushing over the mountain ridge near my home. To run to Him—my shelter in the storm, my refuge, my strong tower—when the enemy of my soul seeks to destroy me. But first I had to realize that He was not only in me but *with* me. What an eye-opener! This realization carried me beyond the veil that obscured my vision of the spiritual realm. It negated the lie that I had been abandoned by the One who promised to never leave me nor forsake me.

Consider this verse: "For in Him we live and move and have our being" (Acts 17:28). *In* Him. Is it possible the Lord is referring to His presence always surrounding us and thus challenging us to open our eyes and see?

Let's put this Scripture in context. In Acts 17, the Apostle Paul was speaking to the men of Athens, a religious center at the time where philosophers abounded. The belief in multiple gods was rampant, evidenced by the sheer number of statues throughout Athens. Despite their overt religiosity, the Athenians were ignorant of the one true God. Their religious beliefs were just that—religious. They had no understanding of the magnificence of a personal God who not only created them but loved them with an everlasting love. Paul set out to open their eyes so that they might see:

> God, who made the world and everything in it, since He is Lord of heaven and earth, does not dwell in temples made with hands. Nor is He worshiped with men's hands, as though He needed anything, since He gives to all life, breath, and all things. And He has made from one blood every nation of men to dwell on all the face of the earth

> and has determined their preappointed times and the boundaries of their dwellings, so that they should seek the Lord, in the hope that they might grope for Him and find Him, though He is not far from each one of us; for in Him we live and move and have our being.
> (Acts 17:24–28)

As I studied these verses, the Lord quickened something in my spirit: Was I guilty of containing His majesty within my own religious constraints, much like the men of Athens? Certainly, I believed He was and is the one true God—I didn't then, and I don't now make a habit of sculpting gods out of sticks and stones. But was I limiting who He is in relation to His children? I had just read that we are to abide *in* Him just as He abides in us. His Word is undeniable: It is in Him that we live and move and have our being. *In* Him. And that is in addition to His Holy Spirit dwelling inside us.

Also, did you catch this phrase in the passage above: "in the hope that they might grope for Him and find Him, though He is not far from each one of us?" When I think of someone groping, I think of someone in the dark who cannot see. They are groping outside their own bodies with their hands extended, searching, feeling around themselves in the dark. Was this another reference to finding the Lord's presence all around us?

Oh, how I needed Him—to know absolutely He was with me. The crushing pain of my husband's betrayal had cast me into a wilderness I didn't recognize. It was dark ... so dark. And cold. And wrought with gripping pain. I could place myself inside this Scripture, seeing myself on my hands and knees, unable to stand, groping endlessly for something. I didn't know what because I was blinded by my circumstances, but I know now I was groping for Him.

I began to wonder what *in Him* looked like and fervently prayed He would open the eyes of my heart to recognize Him all about me. And He did! I began to find images throughout the Scriptures describing the Spirit of God in ways that I could grasp—He walks on the wings of the wind (Psalm 104:3). The clouds are the dust of His feet (Nahum 1:3). His glory and majesty shine as the bright and morning star into my darkness (2 Peter 1:19). I learned His eyes roam the earth looking for those who need to be encouraged (2 Chronicles 16:9). Moses exhorted the children of Israel with these words when they became fearful in the desert: "The Lord your God, who goes before you, He will fight for you, according to all He did for you in Egypt before your eyes, and in the wilderness where you saw how the Lord your God carried you, as a man carries his son, in all the way that you went until you came to this place" (Deuteronomy 1:30–31).

Can you picture the Lord scooping you up in His mighty arms and carrying you when you are too weak to go on? Isn't that beautiful? And this—this is my favorite: "There is no one like the God of Jeshurun [Israel], who rides the heavens to help you, and in His excellency [majesty] on the clouds. The eternal God is your refuge, and underneath are the everlasting arms; He will thrust out the enemy from before you, and will say, 'Destroy!'" (Deuteronomy 33:26–27).

Is He beginning to stir your spirit with understanding? Oh, I pray so!

One of the many stories surrounding Elisha in the Old Testament offers a fabulous example of opening our eyes to find God's presence, protection, and provision in our lives. Imagine with me Elisha and his servant in the city of Dothan found among the hills of Gilboa (referencing 2 Kings 6:8–16).

Elisha's servant stretched in the soft morning light. He rubbed his eyes, grabbed his cloak, and stepped out into the chilly dawn. In the distance, a horse neighed. Then another. He heard the clank of metal. Anxiety swept into his heart, and he turned toward the sounds. His eyes widened with alarm. On the mountainside, hundreds of horses and chariots—a great army of the Syrian king—surrounded the city.

The servant raced to alert Elisha, "Master! Master! They've found you. The Syrians are here. They are mighty in number. Master! What shall we do?"

Elisha lay on his bed. He had been awake for some time, seeking God, entreating Him for the sake of Israel. Though impending danger stood on the horizon, peace stood like a sentinel upon his heart. Elisha answered, "Do not fear, for those who are with us are more than those who are with them."

The servant raised his eyebrows, scrunched his face, and bit his tongue. He knew what he had seen. He knew they were surrounded by a great army. And he knew, no matter what Elisha said, there were a lot more of them than there were of Elisha and him. He might be a servant, but he was no dummy.

Elisha rose from his bed. He wrapped his arm around the young man's shoulder. "Come with me."

Together they walked out into the morning. Elisha prayed, "Lord, I pray, open his eyes that he may see."

Elisha touched the servant's cheek and, with a gentle touch, turned his face toward the mountainside, saying, "Behold."

Then the Lord opened the eyes of the young man, and he saw the mountain was full of horses and chariots of fire all around Elisha.

What are the crucial words here? *Elisha prayed.*

We know he prayed at this moment, but we must assume he had been in prayer long before the battle arrived. Like David, Elisha was a man after God's heart. He knew God well and trusted in His sovereignty. When the battle came, peace stood guard over Elisha's heart. Why? Because Elisha knew the God in whom he believed.

Elisha had learned to abide.

We must do the same.

Abiding in the Lord transitions us to a place where we begin to live within His love, fully aware of His presence surrounding us. But to abide requires action. It's not a wish or a want. Abiding in the Lord requires spending time in His Word, praying much, and sitting quietly at His feet. When we abide in the Lord, our faith grows deep roots that hold when the storms of life come. When we abide in the Lord, we gain an understanding of who we are in light of who He is. We learn His promises. His sovereignty. His character and His covenant.

And when we know these things, our relationship with the one true God is no longer based on feelings, but on truth. Feelings can drive us mad, especially during a crisis when it seems all hope is lost, and God is nowhere to be found. But truth? The truth will set us free from our fears and doubts. Truth will replace our sorrow with joy, our despair with hope. Truth will bind up our wounds and open our eyes to see the One who loves us.

One of the most incredible things the Lord has taught me about His presence—especially when my pain is deep and my emotions tell me I have been abandoned by Him—is the reality of my darkness *is* the reality of His presence. Sounds odd, doesn't it? But please hear me out. Psalm 91:1 reads, "He who dwells in the secret place of the Most High shall abide under the shadow of the Almighty." I believe this Scripture tells us the secret place of the Most High is the shadow of His presence, perhaps better known as the shadow of His wing. A shadow is dark. To be in a shadow requires proximity to the object or person.

According to Psalm 91, when we learn to abide in the Lord—to dwell, to live within His love—our life is carried out in the shadow of His presence. Isn't that beautiful? When I'm pressing into the Lord, when I'm seeking Him with all my heart, when I consistently join Him in intimate fellowship—that's when I'm learning to abide in Him. And when I awaken my heart to the miracle of His presence being with me always, then I can know darkness looming in my life—the encroachment of evil, the anxiety of things happening beyond my control, the torment of heartbreaking circumstances—is not darkness as we know it, but the shadow of His wing.

How do I know this? Because He promised to be with me, even in the bad times, *especially* in the bad times. I can understand that the reality of my darkness is the reality of His presence. He is near to the brokenhearted. He carries us in the wilderness like a father carries his son. God's faithfulness to remain with me is something I know, for I have experienced it.

Have you ever noticed the clouds when the sun is right behind them? They are much darker than the clouds elsewhere in the sky. Solomon said, "The Lord said He would dwell in the dark cloud" (2 Chronicles 6:1). Also, Exodus 20:21 reads, "So the people stood afar off, but Moses drew near to the thick darkness where God was." If you're like me, the first time these verses got my attention, I was astounded. God is light and love and all things wonderful, right? Then why is He dwelling in a dark cloud?

Because of the brightness of His light.

Think of it this way: Imagine with me as an ocean of clouds billows over the mountain ridge. They are growing large and dense as the storm front draws close. It's not long until the bright afternoon sky has grown dark. Are the clouds in and of themselves dark? No. They appear dark because of their proximity to the sun and the density of the water droplets they hold. The brightness of the sun and its angle contribute to the darkening skies.

So it is with God.

You and I are children of God, and yet we all go through periods of darkness. Darkness is not a happy time. Darkness is pain and anguish. But as children of God, we are locked into covenant with Him because of His love. He promises to never leave us nor forsake us. If I understand God is with me, and yet, I find myself in a dark place, is it possible to see the darkness from His perspective and recognize it as His shadow sheltering me? Yes, it is possible because the brilliant light of God's presence overshadows the evil invading my life.

One night, after an excruciating day of sorrow, I lay in bed tossing and turning. Only a couple of months had passed since David left. After entertaining denial on the couch for several weeks, I had taken the bold step of returning to our bed. Perhaps it was too soon. Restlessness overwhelmed me. My thoughts were like an earthquake racking my mind. I wanted to pray but had no words. I felt so alone. Sorrow buried me in a cacophony of silent screams and torments.

*Jesus.* That's all I could pray.

*Jesus.*

I closed my eyes and tugged on the blanket once more. *Jesus.*

And then the most tender ... beautiful ... amazing thing happened. I heard singing. Not out loud but in my spirit. Like a lullaby drifting along heaven's shores came the words, "I will sing over you." Over and over, I heard the melody and lyrics, "I will sing over you."

I felt in awe at the wonder of the Lord. Could He possibly love me so tenderly as to sing a lullaby to soothe my broken heart? Peace settled upon me as I listened and marveled at

His goodness. Then an image came into view. In my mind's eye, I watched as the Lord spread His wing over me and sheltered me from the pain. The image was so clear I saw the wing unfold.

And in the background, the song continued, "I will sing over you."

My heart stopped racing. My tears stopped flowing, and I felt the tension leave my body as I basked in the presence of the Lord.

The next morning, I recalled the incident clearly. As I prayed about what had happened, Zephaniah 3:17 dropped into my spirit:

> "The Lord your God in your midst,
> The Mighty One, will save;
> He will rejoice over you with gladness,
> He will quiet *you* with His love,
> He will rejoice over you with singing."

I realized what I had experienced the night before was the fulfillment of this Scripture. The Lord had been with me in my overwhelming sorrow. He quieted me with His love as He sang a lullaby to His broken child. I found myself in the shadow of His wing where I was safe, loved, and held. These moments are still as vivid to me as the night they happened. God is no respecter of persons. What He has done for me, though it is hard to imagine, He will do for you.

The devotional *Streams in the Desert* has touched my life deeply and granted me much understanding of what it means to abide in the Lord. The following passage from this poignant book speaks directly to what I hope to convey about finding God in our darkest moments—about gaining an understanding of how our crushing pain can illuminate the evidence of God's presence in our lives when we offer it to Him.

> God still has His secrets—hidden from "the wise and learned" (Luke 10:21). Do not fear these unknown things but be content to accept the things you cannot understand and to wait patiently. In due time He will reveal the treasures of the unknown to you—the riches of the glory of the mystery. Recognize that the mystery is simply the veil covering God's face.
>
> Do not be afraid to enter the cloud descending on your life, for God is in it. And the other side is radiant with His glory. "Do not be surprised at the painful trial you are suffering, as though something strange were happening to you. But rejoice that you participate in the sufferings of Christ" (1 Peter 4:12–13). When you feel the most forsaken and lonely, God is near. He is in the darkest cloud. Forge ahead into the darkness without flinching, knowing that under the shelter of the cloud, God is waiting for you. *selected*[1]

When the night of struggle obscures our vision, the reality of God's presence doesn't change. His presence isn't hinged on our circumstances. He is with us always—in the good times and bad. In the peaceful places as well as the chaotic ones. God never changes. He is the constant in an ever-changing world. His Word is truth regardless of what erupts around us. We can trust that His hand is upon us, His arm encircles us, and His heart is touched by our needs.

Always.

# Chapter Three—Catching Sight of the Great I Am

> If we must "feel" God's presence before we believe he is with us, we again reduce God to our ability to grasp him, making him an idol instead of acknowledging him as God.
>
> —Craig S. Keener

Blue tugged on his leash as we passed beneath the pine canopy. Boughs of oak limbs stretched into the arch above us, making themselves known among the evergreens. We stopped along the edge of the country road for Blue to pursue the scent of a critter. As we paused, I heard a crackling sound behind me. It seemed almost rhythmic. I turned to witness an amazing sight—hundreds of oak leaves in shades of burgundy and brown twirling and swirling to the ground. The crackling I heard was the sound made as they bounced from limb to limb and then landed on the road below.

I can't remember ever experiencing this before. Like a multitude of tiny hands clapping, the melody of soft percussion left me speechless. In my spirit, I heard the Lord whisper, *Nan, this is like the joyful sound.*

I stood still, watched, listened, and wondered. There's a verse in Psalm 89 that I meditate on often because I want to understand it. This is the verse the Lord was referring to when He spoke to me:

> Blessed *are* the people who know the joyful sound!
> They walk, O Lord, in the light of Your countenance.
> (Psalm 89:15)

The joyful sound. This verse refers to the tradition of blowing trumpets (shofars) to commemorate sacred events like the Sabbath and holy feasts. The joyful sound of the trumpets ushered the people into a time of worship. I've told the Lord on many occasions I want to be a person who knows and recognizes the joyful sound calling me to worship Him.

And on this quiet country road, He answered that prayer.

By all standards, it was just a walk with my dog down a mountain road. But here's the sweet spot: I love to pray while I walk Blue. I had been praying, asking the Lord for wisdom and direction concerning some personal decisions. I needed His peace, His reassurance. Discouragement's shadow had fallen over me, and I desperately fought off feelings of despair. Then, I heard the gentle percussion of the leaves and turned to watch them dance in their spiral descent to the road. I recognized the Lord's presence—His response to my prayers for peace. And I heard His still, small voice.

The moment became holy as a hush fell over my spirit, and God's peace embraced me.

Holy, as the joyful sound of the falling leaves led me to the throne of grace where I knew I was not alone.

Holy, when I stood still and remembered that He alone is God, and He is worthy of all praise.

My eyes glistened with tender tears. I'd heard the joyful sound calling me to worship, right then, standing still beneath a pine grove with insistent branches of oak mingling within. The light of Christ within me illuminated the evidence of God's presence around me because I had brought Him into my painful struggles through prayer.

Several years ago, I taught the Bible study *A Woman's Heart: God's Dwelling Place* by Beth Moore. This Bible study changed my life. I gained insight that, to this day, transforms me. In this Bible study, I first learned of the correlation between the Old Testament tabernacle—the tent of meeting that traveled through the wilderness with the children of Israel—and us. There is a direct parallel between its design and our faith walk with Jesus. It was in this study the Lord revealed to me how relentless His love and His desire to be with His children are. From this Bible study, I dug deeper, fascinated with the tabernacle's golden lampstand and its function to illuminate the evidence of God's presence in the holy place. I can't wait to share what this has to do with us, especially during times we feel abandoned by the Lord and our faith lies shattered at our feet.

Before we go forward in this study, I need to lay a brief foundation for you. I want you to see and be reminded that we are the temple of the Holy Spirit and the light within us can be rekindled when we willingly offer our crushing pain to the Lord.

The tabernacle served as God's dwelling place so He could be present with His people and they could commune with Him. God spoke these very words in Exodus 25:8: "And let them make Me a sanctuary [sacred place], that I may dwell among them." I love knowing God has always pursued His people with His love. He has always desired fellowship with us, one that was broken through the fall of man in the Garden of Eden.

How can we comprehend that the Creator of heaven and earth wants us to know Him? This holds true not only for contemporary Christianity but also during ancient biblical days. God does not change. He is the same yesterday, today, and forever ... never was He an elusive God. He wants to know and be known by His people.

Perhaps it was through the great exodus from captivity in Egypt that God hoped His people would walk faithfully with Him. Maybe He expected gratitude and wonder at the miracles He favored them with. But it was not to be. An enormous chasm lay between them. He was a holy God, and they were a sinful people—a people given to idol worship because of the influence of those they encountered on their journey. But God did not give up on His children. He was relentless in His pursuit of love, just as He is with us today.

The Lord called Moses to come up to Him on the mountaintop. Moses spent forty days and forty nights on the mountain with the Lord (Exodus 24:18) receiving instructions for a sacred place where God could dwell with His people. The Lord's instructions were precise, down to the cubic inch of each section and the thread color for each curtain. One beautiful aspect of God's instructions was He wanted every part of the tabernacle built from materials willingly offered from the heart.

Say that again with me and let it sink in: *willingly* offered from the heart.

> Then the Lord spoke to Moses, saying: "Speak to the children of Israel, that they bring Me an offering. From everyone who gives it willingly with his heart you shall take My offering. And this is the offering which you shall take from them: gold, silver, and bronze; blue, purple, and scarlet thread, fine linen, and goats' hair; ram skins dyed red, badger skins, and acacia wood; oil for the light, and spices for the anointing oil and for the sweet incense; onyx stones, and stones to be set in the ephod and in the breastplate. And let them make Me a sanctuary, that I may dwell among them." (Exodus 25:1–8)

The Lord designed the tabernacle as a mobile unit that traveled with the children of Israel. It was assembled and taken down, assembled and taken down—all for the purpose of making God accessible to His people. Every detail pointed toward the holiness of God, even His instruction to always place the entrance of the tabernacle facing east. Think about this: The Garden of Eden—a place God specifically designed to have rich fellowship with His people—had an eastern entrance (Genesis 3:24). Also, when Jesus was born, it was a star in the East that led the wise men to the Son of God (Matthew 2:2, 9).

In *A Woman's Heart: God's Dwelling Place*, Beth Moore said:

> God may have had countless reasons for choosing the east as the entrance to His presence; but surely, not the least is the fact that His perfect light interrupts the darkness every morning from the east. At the break of every new day, light shone on the gate to the tabernacle, beckoning the people to find refuge in God."[1]

Are you getting an idea of how intricate God's design is? Are you as awestruck as I?

As we study an overview of the tabernacle, keep in mind its purpose: to serve as a sanctuary where the Spirit of God could dwell in holiness among His people, providing access to Him and a place for atonement of sin and intercession. Every aspect of the tabernacle's design worked to bring the people and their needs before God. As biblical history confirms, and as we'll see in the following pages, the design of the tabernacle also symbolizes our journey of faith to find atonement for our sins, so we might know the one true God.

With the dawning of each new day, the children of Israel had the opportunity to come before the Lord by entering the outer courts of the tabernacle. Passing through the gate embroidered with blue, purple, and scarlet yarns, the often-billowing, white linen curtains that formed the tabernacle walls stood in sharp contrast to not only the colorful gate but also the barren desert surround. A person entering the outer courts of the tabernacle had made a distinctive choice to come before God and express their need for Him, much like we do when we recognize our need for a Savior.

Imagine the sensation for the children of God of stepping onto holy ground the moment they entered the embroidered gate. Everything within this surround had been consecrated to God with the purpose of transforming the individual into His righteousness. Front and center, just beyond the gate, stood the altar of sacrifice—an enormous altar where the Israelites brought animals without blemish to sacrifice for the atonement of sin. In his book *The Tabernacle: Shadows of the Messiah*, David M. Levy describes the moment: "Upon entering the court, they stood in awe, gazing at the bloodstained altar, as the smoke from precious sacrifices curled into the sky."[2] Can you imagine?

The altar of sacrifice, seven and one-half feet square, was made of acacia wood covered with brass. It stood four and one-half feet high. The sacrificial animal had to be lifted onto the altar, just as our Savior was high and lifted up on the cross. The significance of the acacia wood thrills me! Used throughout the tabernacle for all the furnishings as well as the supporting pieces, acacia is a desert tree known for its great strength. It is incorruptible—will not decay—*and* it has heavy, sharp thorns. The symbolism of our Savior's sacrifice astonishes me. We know that Jesus's body never decayed (Psalm 16:10), and because of His sacrifice on the cross. we too will know life eternal, for we have been born again of incorruptible seed through the Word of God (1 Peter 1:23). Throughout the Bible, thorns are symbolic of sin, beginning with the curse that fell upon the earth after Adam and Eve chose disobedience.

The most relevant example of sin to the altar of sacrifice is the crown of thorns Jesus wore during His crucifixion. The fact that the altar for the atonement of sin was crafted from a tree that bore thorns takes my breath away. The Lord instructed the people to place a horn at each corner of the altar to tie down the sacrificial animals. This divine instruction is possibly a nod toward the remembrance of Abraham and Isaac—the ram God provided as a substitute sacrifice was caught in the thicket of thorns by its horns. Also, in Psalm 18:2, David refers to God as the horn of his salvation. That makes sense now, doesn't it, because the sacrificial animal was secured to the horns on the altar. Amazing. The intricacies and overlays of the Scriptures simply astound me.

And now, this is the most significant parallel to our own journey of faith: Although the priests were the only ones anointed to carry out the sacrifice and serve as the mediator between the person and God, the person asking for the forgiveness of sins was required to hold down the head of the animal being offered. This act symbolized "their identification with their substitutionary death on their behalf—their sins were transferred to the sacrifice, and the life of the sacrifice was transferred to them."[3] Wow! An innocent victim, most often a lamb without blemish, lost his life because of the sin of another. Think of the sacrifice on a hill called Calvary when our Lamb of God died for us upon a wooden altar, the cross. It has a new meaning, doesn't it?

I can't leave the altar of sacrifice without one last thought to grab your heartstrings. Again, take note of the thorough intricacy of the Scripture and how the Old Testament undergirds God's plan of redemption.

> At nightfall, Aaron and his sons were to slay and burn an evening sacrifice that God commanded to be left burning on the altar all night. They were to rise early

> in the morning and wait for the last of the ashes to fall through the bronze grate of the altar. The ashes invariably fell at dawn. Ancient Hebrew history records that the moment the last ash fell, the priest blew the trumpets in celebration, shouting, "It is finished!" "When he had received the drink, Jesus said, 'It is finished.' With that, he bowed his head and gave up his spirit" (John 19:30).[4]

Umm ... you can close your mouth now. Isn't that incredible?

Only one other piece of furniture was in the tabernacle's outer court. The bronze basin, also called a laver, stood between the altar of sacrifice and the tabernacle proper known as the inner court. Within the walls of the tabernacle proper was the holy place and the holy of holies. The purpose of the basin was for washing—preparing clean hands and clean feet before entering the inner court of the tabernacle. Only the priests could use this basin because only the priests were allowed to enter the holy place where the Spirit of God dwelled.

The interesting part of this piece is it was sculpted from gleaming brass mirrors the Israelite women plundered from Egyptian women during the Exodus. As the priests prepared to enter the tabernacle proper, it was imperative they be clean before the Lord—to be holy as He is holy, not only physically clean but also spiritually. As the priests bent over the large basin, dipping their cupped hands into the cool water, their mirrored reflection met their gaze. This purposeful moment gave them the opportunity to examine their heart for any lingering sin as they prepared to come before God's presence.

Many theologians believe the bronze basin represents the Word of God for the New Testament believer. Ephesians 5:26–27 reads, "that He might sanctify and cleanse her [the church] with the washing of water by the word, that He might present her to Himself a glorious church, not having spot or wrinkle or any such thing, but that she should be holy and without blemish." The Word of God reveals and reflects our sinful purposes and intentions which must be cleansed before entering God's presence.

The mirrors in the bronze basin served the same purpose as the Word of God—revealing blemishes of the heart. The water, of course, provided the cleansing—the same cleansing the water of the Word affords us. David M. Levy reminds us, "We must respond to the Lord's admonishment, 'But, as He who hath called you is holy, so be ye holy in all manner of life, because it is written, "Be ye holy; for I am holy"' (1 Peter 1:15–16). Only then will we be able to walk through the veil into the holy presence of our Lord and forward into each new day prepared for spiritual service for Him."[5]

Oh, to take this principle to heart if we desire to encounter the Lord once more, as David writes in the Psalms:

> Who may ascend into the hill of the LORD?
> Or who may stand in His holy place?
> He who has clean hands and a pure heart.
> (Psalm 24:3–4)

After cleansing himself, the priest, with great reverence, entered the holy place a short distance away. He parted the exquisite curtains woven of blue, scarlet, and purple threads. Did his heart pound? Was he overwhelmed by the glory of the Lord? Certainly, a hush may have fallen over him as he considered the responsibility of representing the people before a holy God.

A warm glow lit the darkened room while a sweet aroma filled the air. Looking up, perhaps the priest was overcome by the ethereal wonder of the heavens. The ceiling was draped with a luxurious fabric of fine linen woven with blue, purple, and scarlet threads like the eastern gate and the partition separating this holy place from the outer courts. But this drapery was different, being embellished with artistic designs of cherubim. Oh, the sight of the heavenly hosts! I wonder if they appeared to dance before the Lord in the flickering light of the lampstand. Probably not, but what a lovely thought.

The golden lampstand stood to the left side, illuminating the evidence of God's presence in the holy place. Its light burned continually according to the command of the Lord. And the beauty of this? The first fruit of crushed olives—oil that was *willingly offered* to the Lord—daily provided its light. Had it not been for the golden lampstand, the priest would have been in total darkness as the tabernacle proper had no windows, only fabric.

Take a moment and consider this concept: Olives were pressed and crushed to release the oil to keep the light burning continually. This oil was presented as an offering—willingly—before the Lord and provided the light which allowed the priest to see the evidence of God's presence. This offering is the crux of what I believe the Lord wants us to see through the pages of this book.

Let me take you through the rest of the inner court of the tabernacle (the holy place) to give you a full picture and strong foundation for the parallel between the tabernacle and our own faith journey. In the next chapter, we will study the offering of this oil in detail. Are you excited to see what God has for us? He is a good and faithful God who wants us to know Him and His ways thoroughly.

As the priest finished filling the lampstand with the oil, his gaze would catch the table of showbread standing on the right side of the holy place. True to God's explicit detail, the first piece of furniture the holy light illuminated foretold His son, Jesus Christ.

> The term *showbread* comes from a Hebrew word that means *bread of the face* or *bread of presence*, because the loaves were set before the face or presence of Jehovah (who dwelt in the holy of holies) as a meal offering from the children of Israel (Lev. 24:8). God gazed with delight on the pure bread offering that sat continually before his face. Bread is called the staff of life and is emblematic of life itself. The showbread was a foreshadowing of Jesus Christ, who is the true bread of life, giving unfailing sustenance to all that partake of him. He was born in the city of Bethlehem which means *house of bread*.[6]

This table represented the reconciliation between God and man—it was a place of communion between the two.

A bit further into this exceptional space stood the altar of incense. It was placed just in front of the veil that separated the holy of holies from the rest of the inner court. This altar was positioned as deep in the holy place as the priest could go daily. Only the high priest could go further, beyond the veil, and that could only be one day a year—the Day of Atonement. From the warmth of its fiery embers wafted the unforgettable aroma of incense prepared as a perfume, pure and holy. The priest came morning and night before God's presence on behalf of the children of Israel. The incense represented the sweet aroma of intercessory prayer before the Lord.

This altar was a smaller version of the altar of sacrifice that sat just inside the gate of the outer court. The priests used censers (bronze vessels) to scoop coals from the altar of sacrifice, carry them into the holy place, and place them underneath the altar of incense to keep it burning. Only the coals from the altar of sacrifice were considered holy—there had to be a sacrifice before prayers could be brought before the Lord. These holy coals heating the incense to make it a fragrant offering carried the spilled blood of the sacrifice.

A short distance away hung an incredulous, heavy veil woven of the same fine linen with blue, purple, and scarlet threads and embroidered with figures of cherubim. The elegant veil separated the inner court of the tabernacle and the holy of holies. It served as a partition between the priests and God's glorious presence. Can you imagine? How wonderful this veil no longer separates us from our God.

Behind the veil was the ark of the testimony that contained three objects: a golden vessel that held manna, Aaron's rod that budded, and the tablets with the ten commandments—all testifying of God's covenant with His people. On top of the ark was the mercy seat hammered from pure gold. Golden cherubim sat on each end with wings stretched forth, covering the mercy seat. *This* is where heaven met earth—the dwelling place of Almighty God among His people. The Lord spoke through Moses: "And there I will meet with you, and I will speak with you from above the mercy seat, from between the two cherubim which are on the ark of the Testimony, about everything which I will give you in commandment to the children of Israel" (Exodus 25:22).

The holy of holies. The glorious presence of the Lord amid His children because of His relentless pursuit of love—the place of meeting. Beth Moore says it beautifully: "In the earthly tabernacle made divinely with human hands, the ark of the testimony was doubtless the throne of His glory. It was the focus of His dwelling, the seat of reconciliation."[7]

Now through Jesus, the perfect Lamb of God, we can behold His glory also. We can boldly approach the throne of grace. We can draw near to a holy God because He has made us His royal priesthood (1 Peter 2:9). But we must never forget the holiness. Even though we are now the temple of the Holy Spirit, robed in righteousness through the blood of Jesus, we must approach Him with clean hands and a pure heart.

Just as He made a way for the priests to reveal the evidence of His Presence in the holy place by bringing an offering of oil to light the lampstand, so He has made a way for us to discover the evidence of His presence with us. His way, my sweet friend, is to bring the pain that crushes us before Him as an offering. When given to Him, the crushing releases the oil of the Holy Spirit which illuminates the light of Christ and provides a way for us to see the Lord in our midst. With the seeing begins the restoration of shattered faith.

Throughout the remainder of this book, I will refer to the devastation you are experiencing as "crushing pain." We must see the correlation between our emotional pain and our offering of oil obtained through crushing. That's exactly how it feels, isn't it? Thoroughly crushed, barely a breath left.

I want to share a portion of my crushing pain. I wrote the following journal entry several months after discovering the betrayal and destruction of adultery that devoured my thirty-one-year marriage and kept me in a fetal position for months. These words describe the occasion when I experienced God's holiness and restorative power as I learned to approach Him with clean hands and a pure heart in a desperate attempt to put my faith back together again:

Busyness.

Bedlam.

Life moving at full throttle.

Even the cars traveling I-40 on that crisp February afternoon mirrored our chaotic lives. Couple this frenzy with a depleted spirit, fragile emotions, and worn-out body, and you will find me—a woman going through the motions trying desperately to follow the Lord and His plan.

Determined.

Committed.

Dependent solely on Him.

I laid my head against the headrest and, closing my eyes, tried to relax. At last, my friend Marcie and I exited I-40. Fighting for an opportunity to turn left in oncoming traffic echoed my chaos once again. But then ... THEN ...

We passed through the gates at the Cove, Billy Graham's retreat center in Asheville, NC. Without a doubt, we were on sacred ground—ground and facilities dedicated to the glory of God, prayed over and visited by thousands of children of God every year. For sure, the Spirit of God dwells richly at the Cove. His presence is tangible. His peace attainable.

And oh, how I needed His peace.

Marcie and I were there to attend the Asheville Christian Writers Conference. But like our Jewish brothers and sisters say, "Man makes plans and God just laughs!" *Our* plans were to study hard, network sincerely, and capture every moment of a delightful weekend with other writers.

But God's purpose was for me to capture *Him* once again—to let His living waters flow over me. Through my broken places, God was leading me to willingly offer my shattered heart to Him with thanksgiving for His faithfulness and promise to restore.

After dinner, we gathered for a keynote speaker and worship. As the music began to soar, my heart began to melt. I've always loved worship—I've even led it during different seasons of my life. Little did I know that my Father in heaven was about to chisel away at the hard places formed over the past year.

We sang about our wonderful, merciful Savior. We sang about how He rescues the souls of men and offers hope when we lose our way. The focus of the song changed to recognizing it is the Lord we praise and adore, and in moments of worship He gives the healing and grace we are longing for.

All I could see was His lovely face. My adoration lifted me up into His presence as His love came down to meet my life that lay in shambles. His embrace was tender. Kind. I looked into His eyes that pierced my inner being, bringing magnificent light to the darkened corners carefully hidden from others. His consuming fire melted my heart of stone scarred by unbearable wounds.

I felt as though I was living again. Do you know what I mean? The One who loves me with an everlasting love removed the shroud cast upon me by the enemy. I could see a future and a hope—a hope that had once been cast aside as my heart lost its way.

Sweet friend, are you in pain today? Have life's heartaches stolen your joy? Your hope? Your peace? Please allow the Lord to melt your heart of stone scarred by unbearable wounds. Look into His lovely face and let Him search and know you that He might set you free. Take my hand as we go before Him, offering our pain to release His glorious light and reveal His presence. When we feel God has abandoned us, He is close enough for us to hear His heartbeat. L. B. Cowman's insight touched me deeply: "Do not be afraid to enter the cloud descending on your life, for God is in it. And the other side is radiant with His glory."[8] Amen? Don't be afraid. God is with you in the darkness.

# Chapter Four—Emerging from Shattered Faith into the Light

> Faith is the strength by which a shattered world shall emerge into the Light.
> —Helen Keller

This faith walk is quite the journey, isn't it? Especially when the path is overgrown with thorns that stab and unexpected stones that cause us to stumble. Add the darkness of depression or the black torment of fear, and suddenly, the lamp we depend on to light our path grows dim, and we lose our way. Easily. Painfully. Regretfully. But the wonder of it all is that the Lord has prepared a way for us to find Him in the darkness *if* we will seek Him.

Before we explore the structure and symbolism of the golden lampstand, consider this: The Lord Himself is our light in the darkness. In Psalm 27 David declared, "The Lord is my light and my salvation; / Whom shall I fear?" John writes in 1 John 1:5, "This is the message which we have heard from Him and declare to you, that God is light and in Him is no darkness at all." And finally, Jesus spoke to the people and said, "I have come as a light into the world, that whoever believes in Me should not abide in darkness" (John 12:46).

Yes, He is the light of the world and in Him, there is no darkness. We know this, right? But in the darkness of our pain, His light seems diminished. This truth becomes mere head knowledge—it has escaped the heart. We can only see our circumstances, blinding us to His presence.

In the ugliest days of my sorrow and anger, I could not find God. His familiar embrace that had comforted me for years seemed far, far away. The abandonment I felt was real. *Your* feeling of abandonment is real also. This I know. And I'm so sorry. The beautiful thing is as you continue reading, I am going to help you find the Father's embrace once again. This chapter will connect the dots between the golden lampstand in the wilderness tabernacle and us—the dwelling place of God's Holy Spirit.

Are you ready to start digging?

Imagine with me as the priest enters the holy of holies. He has just cleansed himself by washing at the brazen laver in the outer court. Now he is privileged to encounter the Spirit of God. The priest parts the heavy curtains embellished with blue, purple, and scarlet embroidery and steps into the holy place. Before him stands the huge golden lampstand, shaped from one solid piece of gold weighing approximately ninety pounds. Hammered. Beaten. Many scholars believe God intended the gold's brutal beating to represent the sufferings of Christ, who would be wounded and bruised for our iniquities to give us eternal life. The Christ who became the light of the world because, surely, the golden lampstand is a type of the preincarnate Christ lighting the evidence of God in our own lives.

Light from the lampstand filled every corner of the space with a warm, shimmering brilliance. Without it, the priest would have entered total darkness. His eyes must have been drawn to the light, just as God had planned.

Aren't the details of God fascinating? Everything has a purpose. Everything is part of a bigger plan ... even our pain.

I don't like to hear those words, do you? How could a loving, merciful God have a purpose in my pain? Why would He have allowed me to be crushed so deeply—why did He allow the same for you? I don't know. But I do know and have learned this is a fallen world. Bad things do happen to good people. The rain falls on the wicked AND the righteous, and until Jesus returns, this earth is Satan's domain. The promise is God's abiding presence with those who love Him. The promise is Him coming alongside us in our pain, giving us hope in our despair, strength in our weakness, peace in our frustration, and light in our darkness. Regaining an eternal perspective is imperative to awakening our hearts once again. We must remember our time on this earth is but a snap of God's fingers. Whereas everything is monumental to us, the Lord's focus is our eternal life with Him.

The Lord often speaks to me through His creation, especially when I'm hurting and discouraged. Maybe I'm more receptive when the hard-learned lessons come through the beauty of a bluebird or new growth shooting from the demise of a fallen log. Maybe my ears are prone to hear when I don't have my guard up. In my brokenness, the Lord, in His gentle way, reminded me of His light in the context of an offering—an offering of praise given on a cold winter's morning.

I curled up on my couch, coffee in hand. My mind felt numb. My heart guarded. As always in the first light of morning, I watched as the earth awakened. I noticed a songbird perched in the stark branches of the old apple tree, winter still clinging, branches still bare. Her melody, loud enough to hear through the windowpane, rang across the frost-laden earth, warming the atmosphere. A golden halo of sunrise lit up the crest of our mountain ridge with an amber glow and tiptoed across the forest and down the slope, gracing the top of the apple tree—the delicate light illuminating the songbird's feathers.

Light and song.

Winter awaiting spring.

Brokenness crying out for healing.

I listened closely to her morning praise. She sat upon branches bare, oblivious to the harshness of winter, and lifted her voice in song. Was she responding to the golden light?

I remembered times I had responded to the golden light of God's presence, times praise escaped my lips in the winter seasons of my soul. Worship was easy. Songs to the One I loved flowed freely, even in the difficult places. But this time was different. This time my faith was shattered, my life lay crumbled before me, and I didn't know if I would ever recover.

Stark realities of emotional devastation surrounded me. I could sense the Lord lifting my chin to behold His glory, the apricot ribbons unfurling across a lavender sky. I looked away, not wanting to let Him back in. But His light, His love persisted. A song—praise born of great pain—formed whispers on my lips, while tears streamed down my cheeks.

Words saturated with tears—the most precious praise of all. An offering of the highest regard.

The name of Jesus flowed from my lips carried on a melody recognizing my Savior and the beauty of His presence. My chest heaved as sobs broke through the walls surrounding my shattered heart. Cleansing, healing cries. A sacrifice of praise, holy and acceptable to the Lord.

Jesus. The name above all names. The keeper of my soul. At the mention of His name, the light of His presence grew stronger. Clearer. At the mention of His name, I began to find peace. Once again, if only for a moment, I found shelter in the light of His glory. The shelter I was starving for.

I searched the apple tree for the songstress now flitting from branch to branch. She was bathed in the bright light of morning, her song stronger, traveling across the mountain still glimmering with winter's frost.

Her song seemed to expand the light.

*My* song also expanded the light.

The darkened crevices of my once-crushed heart began to find healing in the awakening dawn. The delicate light of Christ illuminated my brokenness as tear-stained praise ushered me into the presence of the One I love, bathing me in the amber glow of hope that I would find joy again—*His* joy. His peace. His fellowship.

I pray the same for you, my friend. I pray you, too, will be healed in Jesus's name.

The first step toward healing is a willing heart, even if we hesitate. Hesitation is okay! God searches our hearts and knows our anxious thoughts ... and He understands. Let's begin by recognizing that the lampstand is the only light source in the tabernacle. Here we find evidence of God's presence: the table of showbread (symbolic of the Bread of Life) and the altar of incense (symbolic of prayer wafting as a sweet aroma to the nostrils of God). When we acknowledge that *we* are the temple of the Holy Spirit, the light of Christ within us *also* illuminates the evidence of God in our lives. The lampstand is a type of Christ.

That's where the offering comes into play.

This is also where we find purpose in our crushing pain.

But first, let's consider the design of the golden lampstand.

Earlier, we discovered the lampstand is hammered from one solitary piece of gold weighing about ninety pounds. The pure gold, having no spot or blemish, represents the deity of Christ. It is a single stand holding seven lamps. Picture in your mind a single shaft with three branches extending on each side, each holding a lamp in the shape of an almond blossom for a total of seven, much like a menorah. Also notable is the golden lampstand was built from a heavenly pattern given to Moses by the Lord.

We find this same pattern and its significance in Revelation 4:1–5:

> After these things I looked, and behold, a door standing open in heaven. And the first voice which I heard was like a trumpet speaking with me, saying, "Come up here, and I will show you things which must take place after this." Immediately I was in the Spirit; and behold, a throne set in heaven, and One sat on the throne. And He who sat there was like a jasper and a sardius stone in appearance; and there was a rainbow around the throne, in appearance like an emerald. Around the throne were twenty-four thrones, and on the thrones, I saw twenty-four elders sitting, clothed in white robes; and they had crowns of gold on their heads. And from the throne proceeded lightnings, thunderings, and voices. Seven lamps of fire were burning before the throne, which are the seven Spirits of God.

The seven Spirits of God ...

Did that jump out at you? The first time I read this, I felt baffled. I'm very familiar with the Holy Spirit, but *not* the seven Spirits of God. This prompted some digging on my part which led me to the discovery of the perfect and complete ministry of the Holy Spirit which is sevenfold and found in Isaiah 11:2:

> The Spirit of the LORD shall rest upon Him [Christ],
> The Spirit of wisdom and understanding,
> The Spirit of counsel and might,
> The Spirit of knowledge and of the fear of the LORD.

These are distinct ministries of the Holy Spirit—ministries available to us once we are willing to light the lampstand of Christ within us by offering our pain to Him.

Apply this knowledge and picture with me the golden lampstand, a type of Christ, the light of the world. The central shaft represents the Spirit of the Lord, its oil feeding the six branches, three on either side, representing the six ministries of the Holy Spirit mentioned in the paragraph above: wisdom, understanding, counsel, might, knowledge, and the fear (reverence) of the Lord. Think of the work of the Holy Spirit in your own life. He gives us wisdom and understanding through the Scriptures. He guides us through His counsel and might to withstand the onslaughts of the enemy. The Holy Spirit also makes known to us the knowledge of Jesus Christ and creates in us a reverential fear and respect for Almighty God.

But if our light has grown dim through brokenness, how do we access the sevenfold ministries of the Holy Spirit? In fact, how do we find the embrace of God we experienced before? We have a sense of abandonment that dulls the senses and dims the light. Walls go up and hearts become hard, no longer pliable in His hand. Is it possible to illuminate the evidence of God in our lives once again?

Now we're getting to the crux of the matter.

How did the golden lampstand burn continually in the tabernacle? The Lord gave Moses detailed instructions for every aspect of the tabernacle. In Exodus 27:20, we learn about lighting the lampstand: "And you shall command the children of Israel that they bring you *pure* oil of *pressed* olives for the light, to cause the lamp to burn *continually*" (emphases mine).

Pure oil was the best, the finest, *the first fruit* of the olive obtained through pressing or crushing the olive. Pure oil held the most value because of its excellent quality. It contained no foreign properties.

What does this have to do with you? With me? John 16:33 has a direct correlation to the principle of the crushed olive. Jesus said, "These things I have spoken to you, that in Me you may have peace. In the world you will have tribulation, but be of good cheer, I have overcome the world." The Greek word for tribulation is *thlipsis*, meaning "pressure, oppression, stress, anguish ... adversity, affliction, *crushing*, squashing, squeezing, distress" (emphasis mine).[1] Tribulation. *Thlipsis* is the same word used in Exodus 27:20 to describe the pressed/crushed olives that provided the pure oil—the oil that lit the lamp to illuminate the evidence of God.

Let me say that again. *Thlipsis* means tribulation. *Thlipsis* is the same word used in Exodus 27:20 to describe the pressed/crushed olives that provided the pure oil!

I almost came unglued the first time I realized this parallel between the Old Testament and the New, especially regarding my struggle. Jesus was acknowledging the walk of faith in a fallen world is not easy; it comes with many perils and much angst. He knew our hearts would often break, and our faith may shatter as a result. But we are to be of good cheer because He has overcome the world and we have access to His perfect peace. Be of good cheer because the crushing event has the potential to rekindle the flame of our spirit. Be of good cheer because, if we can find it within ourselves to *willingly* offer our crushing pain to the One who loves us, the oil of the Holy Spirit will be released to light the lamp of Christ within us. We will find evidence of God's presence once again, *and* we will experience the seven ministries of the Holy Spirit. Up close and personal. Ministries that restore, heal, and awaken our hearts to know the Lord like never before.

As mentioned earlier, one of my love languages with the Lord is through His creation—not in a New Age sort of way but understanding that He is the Creator God, and if we look expectantly, He will teach His goodness and ways through this world He has created. The following is a journal entry I wrote during the time my husband and I were separated. My pain was still so raw I could barely function. I garnered strength each day as I walked along our mountain road, singing and clinging desperately to the Lord. Step with me into these intimate moments with the Lord:

> Finally, after a soaking rain, the sun shone through the crisp blue of an August sky. I rounded the curve near the meadow. My spirit stirred, and I began to sing the lyrics to "I Need Thee Every Hour"—a hymn that has a way of turning my bitter tears to sweet.
>
> *No tender voice like Thine*
>
> *Can peace afford.*
>
> A breeze tousled the canopy of leaves overhead. I raised my face toward heaven, closed my eyes, and pictured Jesus on the cross. I thought of what His great sacrifice meant to me—how His love allowed me to walk hand in hand with the Creator of the universe, how my mind can stay at peace when I think of Him. I thought of the joy He brings amid deep sorrow, and I cherished the hope He offers during devastating despair.
>
> *I need Thee, oh I need Thee,*
>
> *Ev'ry hour I need Thee.*
>
> I sensed God's presence drawing near as peace descended on my troubled mind.
>
> *Oh, bless me now, my Savior,*
>
> *I come to Thee.*
>
> A movement to my right caught my attention. A swallowtail fluttered above the amethyst fluff of a thistle. I watched the butterfly settle upon the sweet source of nectar and, for the first time, realized that its buttery wings were bordered with the colors of stained glass.
>
> Stained glass.

Like a church window.

I've disciplined myself to be alert to God's moments—ever watching for Him, ever listening for His quiet voice. I quickly realized this was such a moment.

Spiked leaves and thorns protruded circularly beneath the purple blossom sitting regally above the thorny crown, its long stem thrusting it toward the heavens. I watched as the swallowtail drank deeply of the nectar, unperturbed I was only inches away. After its long drink, the butterfly rested without fear. Content. At one with its Creator.

The buttery wings with borders of stained glass reflected the Savior's love for me. As if looking through a church's window, I caught a glimpse of Him passing by. Maybe the Lord is with me after all. Maybe, I *will* survive this crushing pain.

*I need Thee ev'ry hour,*

*Teach me Thy will;*

*And Thy rich promises*

*In me fulfill.*

Annie Sherwood Hawks wrote "I Need Thee Every Hour" in 1872 on an ordinary day as a young housewife and mother. She was going about her daily tasks when she became acutely aware of the nearness of the Lord and the joy she had in knowing Him. Several years later, following the death of her husband, Hawkes reflected on her song: "I did not understand at first why this hymn had touched the great throbbing heart of humanity. It was not long after, when in the shadow of a great loss, that I understood something of the comforting power in the words which I had been permitted to write and give out to others in my hour of sweet serenity and peace."[2]

Like many, I am one throbbing heart of humanity touched by these simple words. While walking along this quiet mountain road, I offered up my sacrifice of praise and acknowledged my need for the Lord. My offering opened my eyes to recognize God's presence drawing near.

The following thoughts shared in the devotional *Streams in the Desert* comforted me in my brokenness. Perhaps the words will speak to your heart as well: "Through the trial, we are led to discover the treasure of darkness and the immeasurable wealth of tribulation. We may be sure that He who allows the suffering is with us through it ... Dare to believe He never leaves our trial ... Although His presence is veiled, once we begin to speak to Jesus as if He were literally present, an answering voice comes to show us He is in the shadows, keeping watch over His own."[3]

How beautiful is this truth, and yet emerging from shattered faith requires a process.

# Chapter Five—Treasures from the Darkness of Thorough Crushing

> We want to avoid suffering, death, sin, ashes. But we live in a world crushed and broken and torn, a world God Himself visited to redeem. We receive His poured-out life and, being allowed the high privilege of suffering with Him, may then pour ourselves out for others.
> —Elisabeth Elliot

Elijah. I love this man of God. I find myself tucked away in the words of his life—his passion for the Lord, his indignation at those who would dismiss their loyalty to our God, thinking their way is better than God's. He is brave. Focused. And faithful.

And yet, in 1 Kings 19, we find Elijah running from a crazy woman named Jezebel bent on killing him because he had defeated four hundred fifty prophets of Baal—Jezebel's prophets. Jezebel's god. Do you remember this story?

Under King Ahab's leadership, the children of God had forsaken God's commandments and followed Baal. Elijah called a challenge: "'Then you call on the name of your gods, and I will call on the name of the LORD; and the God who answers by fire, He is God.' So all the people answered and said, 'It is well spoken'" (1 Kings 18:24). So, Baal's prophets did just that; they called on the name of Baal from morning until noon and prophesied until the evening sacrifice. The prophets were running around like lunatics cutting themselves, shouting to their god, jumping, and dancing around the altar they had made.

But there was no answer, no voice. No god paid them any attention.

Then Elijah told all the people to come near to him. I wonder if they were dismayed by Elijah's bold faith, or were they whispering and mocking the man of God? No matter. Elijah had a point to make. He repaired the Lord's altar that had been torn down. He dug a large trench around it, and after putting wood on the altar to prepare for the burnt offering, he cut the bull into pieces and laid it upon the wood. Elijah then told the people to fill four waterpots with water and pour it on the sacrifice and the wood. He instructed them to do this *three* times.

The altar was drenched in water. The trenches surrounding it were also filled to the brim.

Scripture tells us that Elijah drew near and said, "Hear me, O Lord, hear me, that this people may know that You are the Lord God and that You have turned their hearts back to You again" (1 Kings 18:37). And then? "The fire of the Lord fell and consumed the burnt sacrifice, and the wood and the stones and the dust, and it licked up the water that was in the trench" (v. 38). After this victory, Elijah told the people to seize the prophets of Baal and execute them at the Brook Kishon.

Why would I take time to remind you of this beloved Bible story, one I'm sure you are familiar with? Because it is important to our healing and emergence from shattered faith to realize what Elijah did next. After all, he was human too, with human emotions and struggles. He encountered the same pit of miry clay we get stuck in even though he had walked faithfully with the Lord and been an instrument of God's miraculous power.

Elijah ran for his life when he received word that King

Ahab's wife, Jezebel, sought his execution. He ran a day's journey into the wilderness, sat down beneath a juniper tree, and weary from his travels, told the Lord he wanted to die. He said, "It is enough! Now, Lord, take my life" (1 Kings 19:4). Elijah had had enough.

Where was his faith? His passion for God? How could he fall so quickly from the pinnacle of victory?

I've asked myself this before. I questioned everything. I was so disappointed in the Lord and so tired of the constant battles in this faith walk that I no longer wanted to live. I wasn't suicidal, but my zeal for life was gone, and my faith lay shattered at my feet. I had had enough.

I believe this is where these words find you today. I'm so sorry for your loss, your anguish ... your lifeless spirit drained of all light. Everything you are feeling is real. Your pain is justified, your exhaustion and weariness of soul are legit. But I want to encourage you in the knowledge that our God is *El Roi*, the God who sees you and knows all about your pain.

This name of God was revealed in the story of Hagar in Genesis 16. If you remember, Hagar was the maidservant for Abraham and Sarai who fled from the family camp, pregnant and alone in the wilderness, to get away from Sarai's harsh treatment. Verse 7 tells us, "Now the Angel of the Lord found her by a spring of water in the wilderness."

The Lord *found* her.

This implies He was seeking after her in her difficult place.

Just as He does for us.

Another example is found in the story of the woman at the well in John 4. Jesus and His disciples were traveling from Judea to Galilee. As they approached Samaria, Jesus told the disciples to go ahead to get some food because He *had* to go to Samaria. Some translations say He *needed* to go. A Jew would not go through Samaria because the Samaritans were considered unclean. The Jews would walk well out of their way to avoid being near these people. And yet, Jesus *had* to go through there—He was compelled.

Why? Because Jesus knew a woman scorned and shunned by her community would be at Jacob's well during the heat of the day, all alone and thirsty—soul thirsty. He ultimately revealed Himself to her as the Messiah and she believed.

Jesus found her in her difficult place.

And the same goes for Elijah.

As Elijah slept beneath the juniper tree, despondent and wanting to die, an angel appeared with a cake and water, and touched him, awakening him to eat. Elijah ate and then fell back asleep. A second time, the angel of the Lord came, touched him, and said "Arise and eat, because the journey is too great for you" (1 Kings 19:7). "So he arose, and ate and drank; and he went in the strength of that food forty days and forty nights as far as Horeb, the mountain of God" (v. 8).

This display of God's grace and tender watch over His faithful servant always touches me and jerks me out of my own despondency. But it gets even better.

Elijah ends up in a cave to sleep. And the word of the Lord comes to him and asks him why he is there. Elijah answers, "I have been very zealous for the Lord God of hosts; for the children of Israel have forsaken Your covenant, torn down Your altars, and killed Your prophets with the sword. I alone am left; and they seek to take my life" (v. 10). Elijah's despondency is still evident, but I'm thankful he is acknowledging the presence of the Lord. He is being honest with God in his answers.

The Lord told Elijah to go and stand on the mountain before Him. "And behold, the Lord passed by, and a great and strong wind tore into the mountains and broke the rocks in pieces before the Lord, but the Lord was not in the wind; and after the wind an earthquake, but the Lord was not in the earthquake; and after the earthquake a fire, but the Lord was not in the fire; and after the fire a still small voice" (vv.11–12).

Can you imagine? The strong wind howled past the entrance to the cave, shattering rocks as the earth quaked beneath the power of Almighty God. A fire—the consuming fire of the Lord—exclaimed His approval of the life sacrifices Elijah had made through an awe-inspiring display of holy flames racing past the cave's entrance. But not until Elijah heard the still, small voice did he respond. Elijah knew that voice because he knew his God. He wrapped his mantle around his face, went out, and stood at the entrance of the cave.

And they talked.

God responded with gentleness to His discouraged, weary, old prophet. The Lord listened to Elijah as he wallowed in self-pity about having to run for his life after faithfully serving God. God didn't rebuke him. He could have, but He didn't. I think that's because He knew Elijah's heart ... just like He knows yours and mine.

He sees. He knows. And He cares.

Even when we no longer do.

The Lord is seeking you in your difficult place also. Do you remember when Lazarus died? Scripture tells us Jesus wept. He didn't weep because Lazarus had died. Jesus was there to resurrect him. Jesus wept because Mary and Martha, His friends, were devastated over the death of their brother. The Lord experienced the emotions his friends were experiencing. I believe He weeps with us too.

I also believe He draws near to the brokenhearted and those crushed in spirit, just as He promised. But we must look away from our all-consuming circumstances and open the eyes of our hearts to see Him drawing near.

About six weeks after David's affair came to light, and we separated, I won a full scholarship to attend the Christian Communicators Conference. I contacted the director and told her I didn't think I could come. I was barely functional. She encouraged me that my sisters in the Lord would minister deeply to me all weekend and to plan on attending.

David had been communicating with me through email and learned of my plans. The day before my trip, I received an email that sounded like the husband I knew and loved. He was concerned for my safety traveling alone in an older car. He reminded me about our roadside assistance policy and what to do if I had any problems. His words indicated he truly cared—it was a reminder of the strong marriage we had shared.

His words gave me a glimmer of hope.

When I returned home, the kids came to greet me. They all gathered in the living room so I could share. But something was in the air. Tension. Uncertainty. Hesitation. Finally, I asked what was wrong. As it turned out, my computer-savvy son hacked into his dad's phone account and discovered that, while I was gone, David was planning another rendezvous with his lover.

So much for hope. So much for a faith that hopes all things and believes all things.

I fell to the floor and screamed. Groans too deep for words consumed me as I beat the floor with my fist. I couldn't believe it. If a murderer had attacked me and cut my heart from my chest while I was still alive, it couldn't have hurt more. The kids did their best to comfort me, but I was basically numb, curled into a fetal position on the floor.

For a very long time.

I know a woman who lost her son to an overdose. She, too, existed in this numbed state of survival for about three years, trying to come to terms with her loss, trying to understand how a loving God could allow such a dreadful, tragic event. So angry, she refused to accept the love of God for a very, very long time. I know another woman who succumbed to cancer after a valiant fight and proclamation of faith throughout the long battle. Her daughter doesn't understand why God didn't honor her prayers and save her momma. Legitimate questions. Legitimate anger at God. And now this young woman is broken, her shattered faith at her feet with accusations like these: "Where are You, God? If You are so good, why didn't You heal my momma? I thought You were the God who heals!" Real. Heartfelt. Anger destroying a young soul.

In my own recovery, I asked the Lord many questions and thought a lot about a broken heart, and even more about a contrite spirit—*especially* about a contrite spirit. That word had more "oomph" when I considered the condition of my own heart. I learned that the Hebrew word for "contrite" is *dakká*, meaning "crushed, or sometimes to be thoroughly crushed, to be dejected, broken, beaten to pieces, broken into pieces, to be bruised, to be humbled."[1]

The word "contrite" is used often in conjunction with a repentant heart, and certainly, a heart turning bitter toward God needs to be dealt with because the bitterness is *not* of God and separates us from Him just as if we had sinned. But when I found this definition of contrite and began looking at Scriptures referring to a broken and contrite spirit, I knew this word was perfect for describing the condition of my broken heart.

Do you agree? Do you feel like you are broken into a kazillion pieces, beaten up, bruised ... *thoroughly* crushed? Yes and amen! How wonderful to know the Lord understands us enough to provide the perfect definition for how we feel in our crushing pain.

Isaiah 57:15 reads as follows:

> For thus says the High and Lofty One
> Who inhabits eternity, whose name is Holy:
> "I dwell in the high and holy place,
> With him who has a contrite and humble spirit,
> To revive the spirit of the humble,
> And to revive the heart of the contrite ones."

God dwells with us to *revive* the broken and contrite heart:

> "Heaven is My throne,
> And earth is My footstool.
> Where is the house that you will build Me?
> And where is the place of My rest?
> For all those things My hand has made,
> And all those *things* exist,"
> Says the LORD.
> "But on this *one* will I look:
> On *him who* is poor and of a contrite spirit,
> And who trembles at My word."
> (Isaiah 66:1–2)

By faith and through experience, I know God draws near to the brokenhearted and those crushed in spirit to revive us. He *sees* us as He looks upon us. Our pain becomes His pain, our sorrow His sorrow. The Lord knows what it is to be beaten to pieces and thoroughly crushed, and if only we will allow Him access to our hearts once again, the healing will begin.

But welcoming Him in is nearly impossible when we are consumed with questions, disappointments, gut-wrenching grief, and emotional pain beyond belief. Believe me, I know.

My days turned into weeks; weeks turned into months.

Waves of raw emotion crashed over me at the most unexpected times as I tried to process the destruction that had come upon my family. I devoured the Psalms, trying to fiercely cling to my faith if even by just a thread. Psalm 42 became my heart's cry as my tears became "my food day and night" (v. 3). David challenged himself by questioning why his soul was cast down and disquieted within him (v. 5). And then in the honest manner David relates to God, he answered himself:

> Deep calls unto deep at the noise of Your waterfalls;
> All Your waves and billows have gone over me. (v. 7)

Deep calls unto deep ...

There's that intriguing phrase again.

I spoke this phrase repeatedly. I needed to understand its message. One afternoon, I sat on our porch swing, swaying in the gentle breeze, tears trickling down my cheeks. My thoughts surrounded the phrase, "Deep calls unto deep." As unexpected as the song of a bluebird on a cold winter's day, my answer came. It was the Lord's delicate whisper. *Nan, the depth of your pain calls to the depth of My love, and I respond with waves and billows of grace, with tender love and mercy. I want to bathe you in My goodness. My child, I see you and know all about it. I am here waiting for you to let Me in.*

I didn't respond, but I did sit quietly and tried to absorb the magnitude of the moment.

The sun was setting. My shoulders relaxed as I tilted my head back and looked toward the heavens. A river of coral flowed through the sky. The clouds punctuated the dusk like staccato notes in a beautiful melody. But the clouds weren't scattered. Though punctuated, they flowed in the shape of a winding path.

I was reminded of Nahum 1:3, which describes the

clouds as the dust of the Lord's feet. I could picture Him stepping through the heavens along the winding coral path. I could picture Him coming to me in my time of need.

In my desperation, I cried out to the Lord as David did in Psalm 57:1:

> Be merciful to me, O God, be merciful to me!
> For my soul trusts in You;
> And in the shadow of Your wings I will make my refuge,
> Until these calamities have passed by.

He began to quiet me with His love.

But this required me to be still, stepping away from my storm, looking away from the strife within my heart, and remembering He alone is God. Being still and choosing to step away is hard when we are thoroughly crushed and consumed with anger and disappointment toward God. But it is not impossible. It is a decision of the will.

George Matheson said this about Isaac in Genesis 26:

> God's voice demands the silence of the soul. Only in the quiet of the spirit could Isaac hear the garments of his God brush by. My soul, have you pondered these words: "Be still, and know" (Psalm 46:10)? In the hour of distress, you cannot hear the answer to your prayers ... The heart heard no reply during the moment of its crying, its thunder, its earthquake, and its fire. But once the crying stopped, once the stillness came, once your hand refrained from knocking on the iron gate, and once concern for other lives broke through the tragedy of your own life, the long-awaited reply appeared. You must rest, O soul, to receive your heart's desire.[2]

Only in the "quiet of the spirit" could Isaac hear the garments of his God brush by ...

When I consider these words, I am confronted with the goodness of God. In my imagination, I can see His garments flowing and rippling in the gentle breeze of His movement coming to my side. Often in my brokenness, I found myself exhausted from sobs and anguish of heart. Dried up tears. Life sucked out of me. Saturating numbness. But that numb exhaustion made me quiet, and in the quiet, I learned to recognize God's presence drawing near to me.

In the nearness, He began to teach me to look for evidence of His presence. After all, He promised to never leave me nor forsake me, and yet ... I was engulfed in feelings of abandonment when I needed Him the most.

It was during this time the Lord reminded me of the correlation between the Old Testament tabernacle in the wilderness and my own heart serving as God's temple. He revealed I had allowed the light of Christ to grow dim because of suffocating emotional pain. My actions were quenching the flame within me.

Exodus provides God's instruction for caring for the golden lampstand. If you recall from chapter four, the purpose of the lampstand was to illuminate the evidence of God in the Holy of Holies: the table of showbread, the altar of incense, and the glorious veil which concealed the mercy seat of God. The lampstand was the only source of light and required specific instructions of care so that the light would not go out: "And you shall command the children of Israel that they bring you pure oil of pressed olives for the light, to cause the lamp to burn continually" (Exodus 27:20).

Pressed olives. *Thlipsis,* meaning crushed, pressure, stress, affliction, and distress. *Thlipsis*, referring to the tribulation Jesus spoke of in John 16:33: "These things I have spoken to you, that in Me you will have peace. In the world, you will have tribulation; but be of good cheer, I have overcome the world."

Then, as if the Lord Himself sat down beside me and opened my Bible, He led me to Isaiah 11:2:

> The Spirit of the LORD shall rest upon Him,

The Spirit of wisdom and understanding,
The Spirit of counsel and might,
The Spirit of knowledge and of the fear of the Lord.

I prayed, *Lord, what are You trying to show me?* Deep in my spirit, I knew. When the light of Christ has kindled afresh, when the oil of the Holy Spirit is flowing freely in my life, I would experience the Holy Spirit's ministry. I would experience the wisdom and understanding of the Lord, His counsel and might. I would gain knowledge not of this world, and my reverence of the Lord would stream from new depths as I gained an understanding of His sovereignty, love, and abundant grace through my crushing pain. I would find the fullness of God once again. Treasures in the darkness.

*If* I was willing to offer my broken and contrite heart to Him.

*If* I was willing to let go of my pain. I had a right to own it. I was justified in clinging to this atrocious anguish—it was seared to my soul.

But I had to decide to live again.

Are you willing? Are you willing to release the shackles that have you pinned to the dungeon floor of despair? It's dark there—*so* dark. And damp with tears. Cold with anger and disbelief. Outside the prison walls, a fog veils the light of day, its misty cloak concealing what lies ahead. I know. I get it. At least in the dungeon, you have control. Outside the stone wall surrounding your heart, there might be more pain ... there *will* be more pain. That's a given.

Healing begins by calling out to the Lord. Especially if you don't want to. The enemy surely doesn't want you to do this, and your flesh will resist too. We must determine in our hearts that life is worth living, and speaking the name of Jesus, no matter how ugly and messy it may sound, will be like a sledgehammer smashing through the prison chains.

I learned this. As I walked down our country road one summer afternoon, I felt the Spirit of the Lord stirring in me. I knew His voice ... but I didn't want to hear it. I had put Him on the shelf and intended on keeping Him there. But He persisted.

*Call to Me, Nan, and I will answer you and show you great and mighty things which you do not know.*

I recognized the words from Jeremiah. He encountered the Spirit of the Lord while in prison, falsely accused of defecting to the enemy's camp during a perilous time for Jerusalem. During Jeremiah's time of captivity—circumstances beyond his control which surely darkened his soul—the Lord spoke to him: "Call to Me, and I will answer you, and show you great and mighty things, which you do not know" (Jeremiah 33:3). "Mighty things" refers to things inaccessible. God promised Jeremiah that if he would call to Him, not only would God answer him, but He would reveal to Jeremiah great and mighty things that could not be known otherwise—things that would astound him, things that could be considered revelational insight.

I venture to say you are being held captive by your crushing pain, by the broken places that won't let go. You, as I had been, are a prisoner to your emotions that remind you repeatedly God should have intervened but didn't. He could have, but He didn't. If He truly loved you like He said He did, He would have ... but He didn't. Am I right? Those thoughts, those lies, are relentless, hammering away at your faith day and night. Until.

Until you say, "Enough is enough! I want my life back. I want my beautiful faith to rise from the ashes."

I have learned the Lord offers us peace in our place of captivity, which ultimately begins to unlock the door of our prison. In fact, the verses preceding the infamous Jeremiah 29:11, "For I know the thoughts that I think toward you, says the Lord, thoughts of peace and not of evil, to give you a future and a hope," are instructions about how to be set free to enjoy a future and a hope. We will look at this in-depth in chapter eight, but here's a glimpse: The people of God had been carried away captive from Jerusalem to Babylon. God's instructions to them, through Jeremiah, were to "Build houses and dwell in them; plant gardens and eat their fruit...bear sons and daughters—that you may be increased there, and not diminished" (29:5–6).

Be *increased* there, and not diminished! In captivity. But how?

"Seek the peace of the city where I have caused you to be carried away captive, and pray to the Lord for it; for in its peace you will have peace" (v. 7). Seek peace in the place of captivity. Come to terms with the pain. The unforgiving anger. Face the truth that you have been thoroughly crushed and bruised beyond repair ... unless the Lord intervenes. And He will if you determine in your heart to seek peace in the place of your captivity, to rest in the sovereignty of God, to trust those nail-scarred hands once again. No matter how hard it is.

For—"Then you will call upon Me and go and pray to Me, and I will listen to you. And you will seek Me and find *Me*, when you search for Me with all your heart. I will be found by you, says the Lord, and I will bring you back from your captivity" (vv. 12–14).

Did you catch the italicized *Me*? I understand this to mean that when I cry out to God in earnest authenticity and honesty, when I determine in my heart to find peace with my brokenness, I will find the One whom my soul once loved. The blinders will fall from my eyes so I might behold His glory once again. The shackles will release from my arms as I draw them heavenward in praise—tear-soaked praise. I will hear His delicate whispers that had been silent for so long. And my heart will respond with a knowing I am loved beyond comprehension.

When we call to the Lord, He will teach us how to recognize His abiding presence. We will gain an understanding of those heart secrets hiding in the shadows of our inner man. We will be given access to the wisdom of God, and the result will be shalom peace—not the absence of chaos and difficulty, but the experience of contentment and wholeness in the midst of the chaos, difficulty, and broken places.

Great and mighty things will be ours to behold.

Treasures in the darkness.

E. A. Kilbourne shares great insight in a devotion found in *Streams in the Desert*: "You may be tempted to run from the ordeal of a fierce storm of testing, but head straight for it! God is there to meet you in the center of each trial. And He will whisper to You His secrets which will bring you out with a radiant face and such an invincible faith that all the demons of hell will never be able to shake it."[3]

# Chapter Six—Gethsemane's Offering

> Grace comes into the soul as the morning sun into the world; first a dawning, then a light, and at last the sun in his full excellent brightness.
> —Thomas Adams

The ultimate trust.

Deep inner wrestling of the soul.

A song in the wind whistled through the pines. Looking up, I took in the majesty of a September sky. I could hear the wind's song—like a melody played on the strings of a violin. Soft and low. Its moan reflected the cry in my heart, the need for peace and reassurance. I needed to recognize God's abiding presence.

As pavement transitioned to gravel and pastureland spread wide, three bluebirds swooped low, crossing my path. They perched on the rustic, moss-laden fence on the edge of the country road.

My heart leaped at the sight, causing my eyes to lift toward the heavens. God used the blue of their feathers to shift my thoughts to the tabernacle—God's dwelling place. Blue tapestries in the tabernacle were to remind the people of the one true God, the Maker of heaven and earth.

The cobalt blue of the birds did the same for me.

*God, where are You?* I prayed. *Help me find You again.*

The sad song of the violin played through the pine boughs on the gentle breeze. My eyes glistened with sorrow and deep loss, not only in my personal life but in my spiritual one. I felt separated from the Lord. So confused. Accosted deep in my soul by emotional pain.

My eyes scoured the blue sky while my thoughts ran deep. I remembered my tabernacle studies from much earlier in my walk with Christ. The parallels between the Old Testament tabernacle and my own heart being the temple of the Holy Spirit impacted my life with a new level of understanding of God's love.

*Lord, I know You're trying to help me. I am desperate to be free from this prison of crushing pain. Help me understand ... please help me understand.*

As I leaned against the split-railed fence framing a meadow of chicory and daisies, I returned my thoughts to the tabernacle. The only way the priests had evidence of God's presence in the holy of holies was through the light from the golden lampstand. Remember? Its purpose was to *illuminate* the evidence of God in the Holy of Holies.

To be lit required pure olive oil.

Obtaining pure olive oil required crushing.

And *then*, the entire process required a willing heart from the giver of the oil.

A willing heart.

The garden of Gethsemane was a place of solace and prayer for Jesus—a place for Him to call out His greatest needs to His Father. I find it interesting that Gethsemane means "oil press." It was an olive orchard situated on the Mount of Olives frequented by Jesus and the disciples and contained a press for crushing the olives to obtain the oil. This is no coincidence. God is all about the details, even where the Light of the World would be distressed and crushed to the point of sweating drops of blood for the sake of mankind.

Jesus and His disciples entered the garden of Gethsemane following the Last Supper, a Passover meal which, we now know, was ultimately commemorating the Lamb of God—Jesus. The men entered the garden. Jesus became sorrowful and anguished. "Then [Jesus] said to them, 'My soul is exceedingly sorrowful, even to death. Stay here and watch with Me.' He went a little farther and fell on His face, and prayed, saying, 'O My Father, if it is possible, let this cup pass from Me; nevertheless, not as I will, but as You will'" (Matthew 26:38–39).

Three different times Jesus prayed this prayer. Clearly, the struggle to accept the difficult place was real. Yet, Jesus knew from the beginning that crucifixion would be required of Him. He tried to warn His disciples that He would go to Jerusalem to suffer and die. I suppose they couldn't fathom why their Messiah, the Son of God, needed to suffer ... needed to die.

Neither can we. I mean, we can't fathom why *we*—children of God—should suffer immeasurable, crushing pain. Didn't Jesus die to give us abundant life? Didn't He come to heal and save and break the prison walls? Why is our pain necessary? What beauty could possibly come from this? What is the purpose?

And yet, God promises to use all things for my good, to bring beauty from my ashes.

My back pressed against the weather-worn wood of the fence. I wiped the tears streaming down my cheeks and looked up from my thoughts. There were the bluebirds again. It was as if they were following me on my walk, urging me to consider the goodness of God that remains regardless of our circumstances. I desperately wanted all this destructive pain of adultery to go away. I didn't want to suffer through this. I didn't deserve it. I didn't understand it. And I knew my faith was suffering because of it—the promises of God did not prepare me to be destroyed like this.

But then one of the bluebirds swooped to a neighboring tree, perched, and began to sing. The melody was pure and simple, stirring my spirit within me. I sensed God's peace settling on my broken places and strengthening me to press on. I turned toward home with a gentle breeze ushering me along the country road, pondering the ways of God.

It's interesting to me how, without warning and completely unexpected, my thoughts can morph into agony like this. Words, thoughts, and pain spew from my lips as I relive my darkest night, torrents of tears flowing down my cheeks. Perhaps you have been hit by similar tsunamis caused by the destruction in your life. The pain can take our breath away—the pain from betrayal, losing a child, the horrid suicide of a loved one, or a prodigal child to whom you gave Jesus, not just mere religion. The list goes on, amen? We have all been touched by tribulation, thoroughly crushed in its wake. These difficult and broken places eat away at strong hearts filled with faith until the pain surfaces once again.

And we feel as though we can't breathe.

In those moments, even in the reality that my faith had withered away, I instinctively cried out to God. Was it in groanings too deep for words? Maybe. Probably. But God is attentive to the cries of His children. He remains faithful, even when we aren't.

Maybe because I'm a visual learner, I love to consider the God of Angel Armies—the Lord of Hosts. The imagery these words evoke strengthens me in the difficult places. We are not hidden from the Lord. We are not alone in our battle. Though our world has been darkened by crushing pain, His light remains, buried beneath the sludge of miry clay. His eye is upon us. His bottle is ready to catch every tear.

The Lord our God will rescue us if we'll only let Him.

Can you begin to consider the power of God's love that surrounds us with His shield of faith to rescue us from the enemy's grip? He sends out His army of angels to rescue us on our darkest night. Consider the spiritual battle occurring in the heavenly places on your behalf. We are not wrestling with flesh and blood, even though it often feels like it. Our battle is with the enemy of our soul who wants us to waste away in our sorrow and give up living. The principalities of darkness seek to devour us, and they *will* unless we take a stand and make a choice to offer our brokenness to the Lord.

Daniel experienced this.

Daniel was in mourning for the plight of God's people for twenty-one days, praying and fasting, seeking a word from the Lord as he interceded for his beloved Jerusalem. But none came ... until the twenty-fourth day. Daniel was on the side of the great river Tigris when he records, "I lifted my eyes and looked, and behold, a certain man clothed in linen, whose waist was girded with gold of Uphaz! His body was like beryl, his face like the appearance of lightning, his eyes like torches of fire, his arms and feet like burnished bronze in color, and the sound of his words like the voice of a multitude" (Daniel 10:5–6). Can you imagine? The men with Daniel did not see this heavenly messenger, but they were overcome with fear and fled to hide. Daniel was left alone, overwhelmed by the Spirit of God as he fell into a deep sleep.

Suddenly, a hand touched him and said, "Do not fear, Daniel, for from the first day that you set your heart to understand, and to humble yourself before your God, your words were heard; and I have come because of your words. But the prince of the kingdom of Persia withstood me twenty-one days; and behold, Michael, one of the chief princes, came to help me, for I had been left alone there with the kings of Persia" (vv. 12–13).

What an incredible picture of spiritual warfare that occurs on behalf of God's people! It astounds and strengthens me in my fight. Daniel prayed for three full weeks. The angel battled for twenty-one days. Three weeks. Twenty-one days. And *then* the word of the Lord reached Daniel. This passage of Scripture demonstrates answered prayer *and* the power of prayer *and* the battle that is happening in the spiritual realm on our behalf.

Oh, that we could remember this when our emotions consume us and the lies of the enemy cause us to question God's faithful watch-care. He draws near to us in our anguish. He responds to the cries of our hearts. And yet, the feelings of abandonment are real.

As is the anger and disillusionment toward our faith.

Still, we must choose. Will I live, or will I die? Will I seek healing for my soul or not? Will I willingly offer my damaged and bruised heart to the Lord ... or not?

Luke's account of Jesus's prayer in the garden of Gethsemane offers more detail about Jesus's agony of the soul: "[Jesus] knelt down and prayed, 'Father, if it is Your will, take this cup away from Me; nevertheless not My will, but Yours, be done.' Then an angel appeared to Him from heaven, strengthening Him. And being in agony, He prayed more earnestly. Then His sweat became like great drops of blood falling down to the ground" (Luke 22:41–44).

In response to Jesus's prayer, His Father did not remove the cup—the suffering—but He sent an angel to minister to Jesus and strengthen Him. In the agony of Jesus's soul, the Father comforted Him with His tender watch care.

I wonder what the angel did or said. How long did the angel stay? We are not told precisely, but we can surmise the angel strengthened Jesus to endure His agony and withstand the torment of Satan as Jesus confronted the sin that would take Him to the cross. God frequently sends ministering angels to encourage, care for, and strengthen His children in their difficult places—those times when we are overwhelmed by the crushing pain of our circumstances.

We know He is near to the brokenhearted and those crushed in spirit. We also know throughout the Scriptures, God sent an angel to meet the needs of His servants. I can't tell you I physically saw an angel ministering to me in my time of desperate need. Still, surely, they were with me, sent from the hand of God to strengthen His broken, weary, and worn servant because how many times in my distress did I experience unexplained peace? Multiple times, a comfort of divine origin wrapped me in a blanket of love when I least deserved it. The unexpected comfort came in some of my messiest moments when anger and disappointment spewed from my indescribable pain. I believe God, in His goodness, sent a ministering angel to strengthen me to endure. Why? Because He loves me. He knows me. He searched my heart and knew my anxious thoughts, and I believe He understood the anger that entangled my soul while my faith lay shattered about me.

Never forget the longsuffering of the Lord. He does not give up on us.

He seeks after us in our difficult, broken places.

He calls us to come to Him, but our agony of soul forbids it. Surrendering to God's will when it is a billboard for sorrow, defeat, or shame is the last thing on our minds, and certainly the heart rebels against such a ridiculous thought. We experience that deep, inner wrestling of the soul just like Jesus did.

That's why I believe the Lord understands our hearts and struggles so much. Experiencing anger toward God is not a sin. However, harboring it, allowing it to take root and create a barrier between us and the Lord *is* a sin. How did Jesus handle it? He prayed, "Father, if it is Your will, take this cup away from Me; nevertheless not My will, but Yours, be done" (Luke 22:42). Jesus was experiencing the inner wrestling of laying down His flesh to embrace the will of a Sovereign God. "And being in agony, He prayed more earnestly. Then His sweat became like great drops of blood falling down to the ground" (v. 44).

Crushing pain in this life is guaranteed. Matthew 5:45 teaches us that "He makes His sun rise on the evil and on the good, and sends rain on the just and on the unjust." Until Jesus's return, this is a fallen world where bad things happen to good people. Devastating events are inevitable. As the following verses indicate, God warns us suffering will come.

"All who desire to live godly in Christ Jesus will suffer persecution" (2 Timothy 3:12).

"No one should be shaken by these afflictions; for you yourselves know that we are appointed to this" (1 Thessalonians 3:3).

"These things I have spoken to you, that in Me you may have peace. In the world you will have tribulation; but be of good cheer, I have overcome the world" (John 16:33).

Tribulation. There's that word again. It even sounds foreboding when spoken out loud. And yet, Jesus forewarned His disciples with this disturbing word. He wanted them to understand this world is hard, especially for those who are followers of Christ. We are in this world but not of it (John 17:14–16). The principalities of darkness work overtime to diminish our light and influence in this hurting world.

I love that Jesus told them (and us) that "in Me you may have peace." In Him. That's important. Abiding in Christ is where we find our peace. You and I know this. But in our agony of soul, we are no longer abiding there, are we? We have willingly stepped away from precious fellowship with the One who loves us beyond our comprehension. The walls have gone up. The heart has shut down. And we have allowed tribulation, at the hands of our enemy, to score.

In our time of devastation from crushing pain, the enemy

whispers, "God has forgotten you. He has forsaken you. Where was your God when you needed Him the most?" I believe everyone who has a deep intimacy with the Lord will feel this at one time or another. Why? Because we haven't been lukewarm in our relationship with Him. We have loved with intensity. Trusted and applied the truth of God's Word to our lives. That's why when we shut down ... We. Shut. Down. Reverend F. S. Webster said, "God has allowed the difficulty to come upon you, in order to bring you closer to Himself. It has come not to separate you from Jesus but to cause you to cling to Him more faithfully more firmly, and more simply."[1]

Our brokenness has brought us to a place of pure faith. Not feelings of joy and peace and communion. Not walking on rainbows and starry nights. No glorious countenance from abiding with our cup of coffee and Jesus. Nope. We have come to a place that requires the pure faith found at Calvary. Pure faith and a choice. A choice to let the Lord back in. A choice to willingly offer our pain to Him. A choice to accept His hand reaching out in the darkness.

I'm reminded of 2 Corinthians 1:8–9: "For we do not want you to be ignorant, brethren, of our trouble [tribulation] which came to us in Asia: that we were burdened beyond measure, above strength, so that we despaired even of life. Yes, we had the sentence of death in ourselves, that we should not trust in ourselves but in God who raises the dead."

Interesting.

"... that we should not trust in ourselves but in God who raises the dead."

Pure faith.

Pure faith is born in the crucible of our Gethsemane. Just as the oil from the olive is released in the crushing of the oil press, the oil of the Holy Spirit is released in the crushing of our circumstances. And just as the olive oil obtained through crushing served to anoint kings and priests for service, so the oil in our tribulation serves to anoint us for the calling upon our lives—that divine appointment requiring pure faith and a deep knowledge and understanding of who God is. That appointment yet to be fulfilled.

Our Gethsemane supplies the makings of pure faith, but, once again, it's all contingent on a choice: Do we surrender and yield to God's sovereignty, fully trusting Him with the agony of our soul? Or do we clamp down tighter on our right to be angry, our justification in questioning His love? Our rejection of our life of faith?

It's a choice.

It takes a willing heart.

Jesus also had to make this choice, saying, "Father, if it is Your will, take this cup away from Me; nevertheless not My will, but Yours, be done" (Luke 22:42). His offering of pain and willingness to suffer made the oil of the Holy Spirit available to all who would believe. The oil that lights the light of Christ within, revealing the evidence of God to our brokenness, is available. It comes through tribulation, thorough crushing of the heart. But there must be an offering. There must be a willingness to trust, die to self, let go of our justifiable anger and pain, and allow the Lord to breathe on us and rekindle the flame. The light of Christ within us has grown dim beneath the weight of the crushing pain. There must be an offering of anguish to allow the oil of the Holy Spirit to light the dying wick within our hearts.

On one sleepless night, I wrestled with this. Repeatedly, I asked the Lord, "Where is Your light? Complete darkness shrouds me. *Where* is Your light?" My accusations were harsh yet honest. I didn't have the desire to play the self-righteous game.

Through the bedside window, I could see the inky jet of night blanketing the earth in deafening silence. Stillness. Thorough darkness matched the thorough crushing of my heart and spirit. Although a billion stars scattered tiny points of light high above me, the complete darkness outside my window remained—heaven's light was out of view.

Much like my own inward light.

I merely existed, walking numbly through each day waiting for the next one to come. The darkness outside my window reflected my thoughts—thoughts of discouragement and depression. When did I let go of hope? And when did I start focusing on the darkness and not on the face of my God? That wasn't like me. I assume it isn't like you either. But nevertheless, here we are.

I often thought about the tiny points of light high above me, out of view, and considered a favorite image from Job 38:7:

> When the morning stars sang together,
> And all the sons of God shouted for joy.

Were the morning stars heralding the coming of the dawn, joining voices with the angels around the throne of God—even in this darkness outside my window and in my heart?

It's possible, especially in my imagination.

But I think there's more to it than that. As I lay there staring at the darkness outside my window, I considered the ways of God and the words of Job who surely would understand my plight.

Just before the dawning of each new day, a bright light appears in the eastern sky—the morning star. It's brighter than all other stars and appears when the night is at its darkest, just before our Creator God paints the heavens with ribbons of apricot and splashes of lavender celebrating the rising of the sun.

The morning star.

Perhaps the stars of the morning were singing to proclaim the presence of *the* morning star breaking through the darkness in the eastern sky. Jesus said He is the Morning Star: "I am the Root and the Offspring of David, the Bright and Morning Star" (Revelation 22:16). And Peter gave us more information: "And so we have the prophetic word confirmed, which you do well to heed as a light that shines in a dark place, until the day dawns and the morning star rises in your hearts" (2 Peter 1:19).

Isn't that like Jesus to break through our darkness at just the right moment and draw us into His marvelous light? That's what He did for me in those difficult, darkened days. He opened my eyes so I might see Him and whispered with His delicate voice until His love rose in my heart—that reassurance all was well with my soul, reassurance He holds the whole world in His hands and even catches the sparrows when they fall. He reminded me that He is *El Roi*, the God who sees me and knows all about it.

What if the stars didn't sing in the morning light to herald His dawning? What if *I* don't sing His praise in my darkest hours? Is He still there? Will He come to my aid and rescue me from the darkness?

And what if I can't bring myself to lay down that which has broken me on His altar of love, willingly bringing the oil from the crushing pain to Him to light the evidence of God within me? What if I can't do that? What if you can't? Does that mean His light is no more? Does it mean His light is no longer within me? Within you? No. He remains regardless of our actions. His presence with us is not contingent on our attitudes or heart condition. His presence with us is contingent on His promise to never leave us nor forsake us.

Even if we feel otherwise.

But without the oil for the light, the *evidence* of God is hidden in the darkness.

Our offering of "not my will, but Thine be done" places the oil for the light into the hand of the One who calls us His own. Though the darkness falls about us, He is there, waiting—waiting for the perfect moment to break through the ebony of night and spill His brilliant light over all that pertains to us.

He is waiting for us to give it all to Him.

I feel compelled to pray with you at this juncture—this place of decision. It's not easy to let go, and you should not do it for anyone else but yourself. This is your pain. You own it. But oh, the freedom that comes with letting go. The shackles fall from our hearts, and we can live again.

*Father, only You can understand the depth of my pain, only You can set me free as I yield to You. I don't want to let it go ... and yet, I desperately do. If I let go, does that mean the injustice, the death of my child, the betrayal of my husband or friend, or the untimely death of my loved one doesn't count? Because, Lord, it does count! My heart is wrapped in the reality of that pain.*

*Help me let go. Help me offer it to You—so You can heal and restore me to fellowship with You—so You can help me live again. In some ways, I'm afraid to let go. The pain has become such a part of who I am. Help me find my identity in who You are, not define myself by this agonizing pain. Give me the courage to continue this journey to healing. Make me brave, Lord ... make me brave.*

*Truly, I love You, but I am so disappointed in You. Please forgive me, Lord. Help me see things through Your eyes, through the lens of eternity where it could possibly make sense. Awaken my heart to love You once again. In Jesus's name, I pray. Amen.*

## Chapter Seven—When Shackles Fall

> Choose to live, not just breathe. Live. Even through the pain and the unexplained. Accept an end so you can begin again. It's not over for you.
> —Beth Moore

Two years, three months, and five days. That's how long David had been staying in an extra bedroom upstairs after returning completely homeless in October 2016. It was hard to believe so much time had passed without reconciliation. We were like two roommates sharing a roof but living separate lives.

I often thought back on how he had walked and hitchhiked for two days to return to our beloved mountains. I knew the night of his arrival something was very wrong, but I still did not want him here. October chill or not. Walking or not.

I sent him away.

My memories of that night, how my son passed his dad walking along the road, are still vivid. It was nine o'clock in the mountains. In October. A cold night. My son picked him up and brought him home. The homeless shelter was full, so I agreed he could stay upstairs for a couple of weeks until he found a job and an apartment. A couple of weeks ...

And although two years, three months, and five days later, he remained, now we knew the culprit that started this entire mess: frontotemporal dementia (FTD). David had just been diagnosed and finally ... *finally*, we had an explanation. FTD presents itself with a personality flip and bizarre, inappropriate behaviors. The victim of this disease loses the ability to reason and make good and bad judgments.

And it's terminal.

*And* he had no one to care for him but me. His extended family had also disowned him because of his indulgent, destructive behaviors. Before you think I am sweet, compassionate, and saintly, think again. I did not want him in my home.

That's the thing about adultery. The damage is so deep and painful that the thought of returning to life as it had been is not on the radar. It isn't a thought, a wish, or even up for discussion. This was *my* broken heart, *my* uprooted life, and it was *my* pain to own and define myself by.

But now ... how was I going to handle this? Clearly, David couldn't take care of himself. In fact, that's what led to the testing that discovered FTD: Something was very wrong. Finding a job and an apartment for him was not an option. At the same time, I couldn't allow him to die alone under a bridge.

One stormy afternoon as I passed through my home office, I abruptly stopped. I could sense the Spirit of God stirring within me. It had been quite a while since we had shared any semblance of conversation—I had Him tucked away in His proverbial box on a dusty shelf.

But I still knew His voice.

*Nan, will you take care of My faithful servant?*

*Ummm* ... that *would be a no!*

*You don't have to, but he has no one to look after him.*

My gaze shifted to the window where trees were blowing from a storm coming up over the mountain ridge. I walked over, placed my folded arms on the windowsill, and stared as sheets of rain began to fall. I wish I could tell you tears of compassion began to fall that mimicked the torrents of heavenly tears outside my window.

But they didn't.

*How can You ask me such a thing, Lord? I don't even want to be in the same room with him, and You think I should take care of him ... indefinitely? I don't think so.*

God gave me a silent space as I wrestled with the devastation of the previous four years. No doubt I still loved the man I had married, but I did not know the man he had become, and my heart could not take much more.

Still, I experienced a soothing balm as the Spirit of God surrounded me—not with a persistent prodding, but with a loving knowing of how hard His request was for me.

The storm outside my window retreated, leaving a gentle breeze in its wake. It blew through the open window and whisked past my face, gently drying my tears.

*If I agree to this, Lord, You had better help me. I cannot do this in my own strength. And grace ... I will need enormous amounts of grace. You are asking so much of me! You know I still love You, don't You? I do. But I'm so stinking mad at You for letting this happen to us. And yet, here You are wiping my tears once again.*

*So is your answer yes?*

*Yes, Lord. I'm saying yes, but clearly this is Your will and not my own.*

I don't recall any sweaty drops of blood during that tug-of-war, but as I stood at the window watching the storm, I thought of Jesus in the garden of Gethsemane when He, too, chose God's will over His own.

The devastation in my heart is no different from the devastation in yours. Different circumstances, yes, but the same crushing pain. It's eating you alive, isn't it? The anger and disappointment you are feeling toward the Lord have sucked the life out of you. I know. I get it. But here's the thing: His love remains. His presence abides. Just as Jesus wept when Lazarus died because of Mary and Martha's pain, I believe He sheds tears for you. I believe He longs for reparation in your relationship with Him.

I found it begins with a willing heart—a willingness to offer the crushing pain that almost destroyed us. When we make the difficult decision to bring our brokenness before Him as an *offering*, something powerful begins to happen. This is when the shackles fall.

An offering is a sacrifice—a giving of something of great worth. Our broken hearts have great value to us; it's our pain to own. We are justified—entitled to it. That is, I believe, why the Lord calls our sacrifice an offering. In His mercy, He understands the profound difficulty which comes with letting go—surrendering that which has consumed us.

He understands how difficult it is to trust Him at this juncture.

I can look back now and know that the Lord was preparing me for this time when I would need to empty my heart before Him, letting go of the destruction of adultery. I mentioned earlier my brother committed suicide in March of 2003, and six weeks later my daddy was diagnosed with leukemia—seven months later he died. I had not told you my mom passed away when I was twenty. I was a brand-new Christian believing God could do anything—just like a child trusting her daddy. But Mom died. And I learned. And my faith grew roots. But now, with the death of my brother and father, my immediate family was gone. The fires of adversity were so intense, I thought I would surely drown in my sorrow.

I remember standing at the kitchen sink washing dishes. The suds billowed and the water streamed, reflecting the tears flowing down my cheeks. My tears had been bottled up for so long, I couldn't seem to control them any longer. I was tired. Weary. Worn.

From deep inside, I heard the Lord's quiet whisper: *Come to Me, Nan.*

My shoulders shook with sobs. I was angry with the Lord, disappointed ... numb, and all the above. I scrubbed the dishes harder, trying to push His voice away.

In His tenderness, the Lord spoke to me again, *Come to Me, Nan, and rest.* This time I listened.

*I'm coming, Lord.*

I dried my hands and shuffled to my study. There, I knelt by the loveseat and began to cry. Groans too deep for words spewed from my lips.

*Give it to me, Nan. All of it. Your heart has grown stagnant with debris that is blocking My living water from flowing. I want to heal you and repair the broken places, but there's no room for Me until you empty your heart of the stagnant water.*

That unleashed the dam.

My cries became gut-wrenching. I offered the desperate regret and confusion over my brother's suicide—the extreme loss. I told the Lord how my dad's death, especially so soon after Don's, seemed unfair and unnecessary. Hidden sorrow over my mom's death all those years ago rose to the surface and met the Savior's love.

I heard the Lord whisper again, *Go deeper, Nan ... empty your heart before Me.*

I sat quietly before Him and things began to bubble to the surface—wounds so deep I had them tucked away in dark crevices of my heart. My secrets. My wounds ... my business and no one else's. But now they rose to the surface: molestation as a child by my brother's friend, religious people in the church who stabbed us in the back, a prodigal child, and extreme financial need due to unemployment. One by one, I spoke their names and gave them to the Lord.

At last the dirty, stagnant water in my heart was gone. Exhaustion crept in as I sat quietly before the Lord. Broken pieces lay in my heart, but they were no longer covered with stagnant water—they were now exposed to the light of the Lord.

*I want you to praise Me, Nan. Don't praise Me for your loss. Praise Me for who I am. Your praise will turn the valve that releases My living water. It will flow through you and bring you healing and hope and peace.*

I began to praise. Slowly. Yet surely.

"I love You, Lord. You are my Rock and my Redeemer. You are the Mighty God who set me free. My Deliverer and Friend."

I felt the rush of living water deep in my spirit.

"You are my Strong Tower. I run to You and find safety. You are *Jehovah-Jireh*, my Provider. You are *Jehovah-Rapha*, my Healer. You are *El Roi*, the God who sees me and knows all about it. I lift Your name on high, Lord. You alone are worthy of my praise."

The weight began to lift. The healing balm of Gilead surrounded my broken places. His peace blanketed me with love. And though sadness still followed me for some time, my willingness to offer it to the Lord sustained me.

I carried that lesson with me for a long time—the lesson of answering the Lord's call to come to Him when I am weary and worn ... until I didn't.

Fourteen years later, and here I am again, except this time not only was there great sorrow but also deep-seated anger and disbelief that my God did not prevent this devastation to my heart. The enormous divide I experienced in my relationship with the Lord is, I suppose, what you are going through now. You have presumably surrounded your heart with the walls of a fortress with no windows to let light in, especially the light of Christ. God has let you down and you are done.

Except you're not.

Out of the emptiness of your heart comes a longing that you cannot extinguish—a longing to be restored, to live again. You want to breathe, to laugh, to dance just for the fun of it beneath the stars. But you can't find your way out of the darkness. You desperately want the shackles to fall from your spirit and set you free. You want to take the hand of Jesus and walk with Him again.

But it seems impossible. How is a hardened heart softened? How is a flame rekindled when tears flow and bitterness abounds in the shadows?

I know how hard this is. Your spirit is crying out for *Ruach*, the breath of God that brings life, but your flesh is not ready. The anger and bitterness don't want to let go. But you must. You must come to a day of reckoning if you no longer want to be consumed by this deadly poison. This is *your* life—you are not defined by what has happened. You have value. You are worthy of joy and peace ... you are worthy of freedom from these chains.

Are you familiar with the Serenity Prayer? "God grant me the serenity to accept the things I cannot change, the courage to change the things I can, and the wisdom to know the difference." This was written by a Lutheran theologian, Reinhold Niebuhr, in 1932. In 1951, he changed it to say, "God give me the grace to accept with serenity the things I cannot change ..."[1]

The *grace* to accept with serenity. Peacefulness. Calm. Composed and content. Grace to accept with serenity the things we cannot change. The act of adultery cannot be changed, but my response to it can be. The bitterness of your divorce is real and destructive. It happened, and it *was* bitter, but together, you and I can change your heart's response. Your child *did* die. Senseless. Sorrow beyond description. Emptiness beyond filling. It happened, but you can't change it. You can, however, come to a place of acceptance that will make the shackles fall, and you can keep the memory of your child alive with joy and great love.

Only by God's grace can we find the serenity—the peace—to accept the things we cannot change. Second Corinthians 12:9 reads, "And He said to me, 'My grace is sufficient for you, for My strength is made perfect in weakness.'" What is God's grace, this promise of sufficiency for anything we may face? We know it as God's mercy, compassion, and unmerited favor. But let's go deeper. *The New Strong's Exhaustive Concordance of the Bible* tells me that the word used for "grace" in this Scripture is *charis* (khar'-ece), meaning "the divine influence upon the heart, and its reflection in the life."[2] It is God who works all things together for our good. It is God who holds our broken hearts in His capable hands and puts them back together again. It is God whose grace *is* sufficient, for He is *El Shaddai*, the All-Sufficient God. His sufficiency meets our insufficiency and makes us complete. Our sufficiency comes from Him.

The Lord has a divine influence upon our hearts... if we'll let Him.

Henri Nouwen, a twentieth-century Dutchman, Catholic priest, and gifted preacher, taught that through our own brokenness, we are deeply loved by God. In his book *A Cry of Mercy*, Nouwen said, "Take my tired body, my confused mind, and my restless soul, into Your arms and give me rest, simple quiet rest."[3] Sounds lovely, doesn't it? Oh how the Father longs to do this for us. *God give me the grace to accept with serenity the things I cannot change, the courage to change the things I can, and the wisdom to know the difference.* It's up to us to be willing to work on those things we want or need changed. No matter how impossible it seems.

Before the heart is willing to offer the crushing pain to the Lord, we must seek the simple quiet rest Henri Nouwen spoke of. Until we desire to put down our boxing gloves or lower the accusing finger ... until we quit the fight and let down our guard, God's rest will remain elusive.

The Lord promises to be merciful to us. I believe He waits for a repentant heart, so He will be exalted, and we will experience His grace. Yes, our God will wait for us. He is longsuffering, merciful, and kind. He waits for us to return to Him with our whole heart, soul, mind, and strength. He waits. And while He waits, we learn He alone is our hope. Our joy. Our peace.

> For thus says the Lord GOD, the Holy One of Israel:
> "In returning and rest you shall be saved;
> In quietness and confidence shall be your strength."
> But you would not. (Isaiah 30:15)

But you would not ...

Or maybe ... just maybe, you're ready to say yes to His whisper to come.

"Take my tired body, my confused mind, and my restless soul, into Your arms and give me rest, simple quiet rest."

Isaiah 28:12 reads,

> To whom He said, "This is the rest with which
> You may cause the weary to rest,"
> And, "This is the refreshing."

The Hebrew word used for "rest" in this passage is *menuchah* (meh-noo-*chah*), meaning "place of stillness, repose, consolation ... a quiet place." [4] *Menuchah* is also used in Psalm 23:2, "He leads me beside the waters of *menuchah* [the waters of quietness]."[5] The waters of rest.

Quiet waters are not troubled or turbulent. They are still. Calm. We can see reflections in them. When we yield to the Father and allow Him to lead us beside the waters of *menuchah*, we learn to be still, cease striving, and remember He is God. We can see His reflection in our waters of quietness—we are able to recognize His nearness.

The choice is ours.

Wounds of the heart can grow bitterness. Ugliness. Anguish, distress. Or heart wounds can grow good seeds of grain, crushed to produce life-giving bread to feed others. Deep faith can grow with roots steady and strong. Eyes can open to see abundant grace and the abiding presence of the Lord.

When God spoke through Isaiah about the *menuchah* rest and refreshing, the Lord ended verse 12 with "Yet they would not hear." I don't want to be that person who will not hear the word of the Lord. I don't want to be so stubborn ... and proud ... that I miss the healing, rest, and the refreshing God has for me. But I've been there. I've been that stiff-necked girl. I felt so entitled to my pain I didn't want to let it go. I believe this is where your heart may be now. And yet, here you are, clinging desperately to the hem of His garment, yearning for healing and restoration. Oh, the conflict between flesh and spirit!

God is pursuing you just as He pursued me. When I finally stopped running, His mercy and grace, so undeserving, washed over me, mingling tears of great sorrow with tears of thankfulness that the Lord my God loved me still and remained faithful. Even in my ugliness—He loved me still. Just as He loves you. Relentless, everlasting, thorough, and complete love.

Have you ever studied storm clouds, especially the ominous ones painted in a deep charcoal color that billow and roll as they march toward your home and community?

Have you ever considered the sun is still there, hidden behind the storm? It is. This is an important point to take hold of. God remains in our life's storms. Exodus 19:9 reads, "And the Lord said to Moses, 'Behold, I come to you in the thick cloud, that the people may hear when I speak with you, and believe you forever.'" Likewise, 1 Kings 8:12 tells us, "Then Solomon spoke: 'The Lord said He would dwell in the dark cloud.'"

Thick cloud. Dark cloud. A thick cloud of darkness.

We often perceive the darkness in our lives as an absence of God. But Scripture tells us that God *dwelled* in a dark cloud, the very light of His glory casting a shadow on the cloud. As a child of God, we are never abandoned by God. Is evil personified as darkness in life? Yes, of course. But we are not of this world. Our God is with us always, and the immediate darkness we experience is the shadow of His presence shielding us, drawing near to us in our difficult places.

When our hearts are hardened from our emotional pain and great loss, our darkness *feels* evil. The operative word here is "feels." God's Word tells us otherwise. God's Word promises that He draws near to the brokenhearted and those crushed in spirit. He is in the storm cloud that has descended upon your life, stripping you of breath. He has been with you all along. Just as the sun remains when the storm cloud passes by, so the Lord remains faithful to us. But will we hear? Will we open our eyes to see?

A quote attributed to F. B. Meyer, a pastor and evangelist in England during the early twentieth century, goes, "As we pour out our bitterness, God pours in His peace." But how? I believe we find peace once again when we recognize the evidence of His presence in our brokenness as we break free and the shackles fall. I've learned this requires an offering—an offering of worship from a willing heart, though battered and torn, a heart that longs to see Jesus once again.

Do you remember our discussion of the golden lampstand from earlier? Exodus 27:20 reads, "And you shall command the children of Israel that they bring you pure oil of pressed olives for the light, to cause the lamp to burn continually." The lamp was to burn by consuming a continuous supply of oil. Do you also recall the Old Testament tabernacle is a parallel to our bodies, as believers, being the temple of the Holy Spirit? Christ in us illuminates the evidence of God in our lives. He is our lampstand. The light of the world. Through His agony of the decision in Gethsemane and His crushing pain on the cross, He symbolically went through the olive press to provide the oil of the Holy Spirit for us. At our moment of salvation, the Holy Spirit is given to us so we, too, may become the light of the world (Matthew 5:14). In this the Father is glorified.

I love the insight Beth Moore shares in *A Woman's Heart: God's Dwelling Place*: "Although that light can never be extinguished, the brightness of our flame entirely depends on how much oil (the Holy Spirit) we allow Christ to pour on us ... The Holy Spirit came to fuel it perpetually. If we do not burn with a passionate flame, it is because we have limited God, who prepared us for victory. Paul warns us: 'Do not put out the Spirit's fire'" (1 Thessalonians 5:19).[6] Do not quench the Spirit.

Unresolved anger will quench the Spirit.

Bitterness will all but extinguish the flame.

But when our crushing pain is offered to the Lord from a willing heart, the spark is rekindled. The oil of the Holy Spirit begins to flow, and the breath of God breathes on our struggling, stifled spirit, igniting the flame once again. With His light encountering our darkness, the evidence of His presence, though hidden in our hardened hearts, is illuminated within us. Our remembrance of Him becomes sweet. Long-forgotten faithfulness speaks in remembrance from the darkened crevices of a broken heart. His voice, once shunned, gives reassurance of His great love.

My healing came in stages. Long before I could agree to care for my husband, the Lord pursued me—just as He is pursuing you now. One of the pivotal moments came on a Sunday morning at church. The morning rain saturating the mountain dispersed, and the sun began to break through the remaining clouds. A beam of sunlight streaked across the sanctuary and bounced off the wooden cross behind the pulpit. Hope reflected. Healing reminded.

The preacher read the sermon text from Luke 7:36–38:

> Then one of the Pharisees asked Him to eat with him. And He went to the Pharisee's house, and sat down to eat. And behold, a woman in the city who was a sinner, when she knew that Jesus sat at the table in the Pharisee's house, brought an alabaster flask of fragrant oil, and stood at His feet behind Him weeping; and she began to wash His feet with her tears, and wiped them with the hair of her head; and she kissed His feet and anointed them with the fragrant oil.

Jesus had done a remarkable work of forgiveness and restoration in this woman's life. With unabashed thanksgiving, she knelt before Him and offered that which had great worth—an alabaster flask of fragrant oil to anoint His feet bathed in her grateful tears. The sweet aroma of worship wafted toward heaven.

The preacher spoke of her act of worship, her gesture of humility. He spoke of her offering to the One she loved—how she fell at His feet much as we fall at the foot of the cross to receive His mercy and grace. As the preacher spoke, I felt my spirit stirring within me. The Lord beckoned me to the altar to give Him that which was of utmost worth to me—my broken heart.

I knelt on the crimson carpet, tears washing away residual anger and confusion. In my mind's eye, I looked at the face of Jesus. His eyes searched mine. And He smiled.

I reached deep into my heart and wrenched the roots of betrayal's destruction away—away from the new work my God was doing in me. Away from tender scars still vulnerable to the enemy's taunts. I handed Him the dirtied roots. Thankfulness rose like a flood in my parched spirit as my healing continued.

I wonder if the woman restored from a broken life felt compelled—*drawn*—to the feet of Jesus to express her gratitude. Did her heart respond unashamedly to the love of her Savior? In that moment of worship, was she aware of the others in the room, or was she so enthralled with Jesus that, at that moment, her focus was Him and Him alone?

I personally believe she was compelled. Unashamed. And enthralled by His love and amazing grace. I know I was. And am. And always will be. This is what the offering of your pain can do for you as well ... over time. It is a journey. Long, arduous, and almost certainly difficult, but the reward is great. *He* is our exceedingly great reward.

As I knelt that day before the Lord with my grateful tears and offered the roots of betrayal's wounds, His eyes took my breath away. Through His radiant light, I remembered hope and reached for healing.

> "Thus says the Lord: 'Again there shall be heard in this place—of which you say, "It is desolate, without man and without beast"—in the cities of Judah, in the streets of Jerusalem that are desolate, without man and without inhabitant and without beast, 'the voice of joy and the voice of gladness, the voice of the bridegroom and the voice of the bride, the voice of those who will say:
>
> "Praise the Lord of hosts,
> For the Lord is good,
> For His mercy endures forever"—

> *and* of those who will bring the sacrifice of praise into the house of the LORD. For I will cause the captives of the land to return as at the first,' says the LORD." (Jeremiah 33:10–11)

You have been held captive, shackled by the betrayal, injustice, pain of loss that nearly killed you, but God is setting you free ... if you'll let Him. He sees. He knows. He cares. Freedom does not dismiss what you have suffered. Freedom gives you control and will bring you life again.

May I pray for you?

*Lord, You are mighty to save, to deliver me from all my troubles. You hung the stars in place, You tell the ocean how far it can come—nothing is too hard for You; You do all things well, and yet, my suffering remains, my heart hurts, and my mind drives me crazy with restless thoughts. Where are You, God, when everything falls apart?*

*I know when I release praise from a pent-up heart, I will find You. Forgive me, Lord. Forgive me for taking my eyes off You. Forgive me for forgetting Your faithfulness. Your mercy and grace sustain me. Your compassion undergirds me with tender care. Your presence strengthens, protects, and guides me through these difficult days. You alone are worthy of praise.*

*I have come to know that even when I can't trace Your hand—when I don't understand my circumstances—I can always trust Your heart. Always.*

*And for that, I give You praise—not for my circumstances, but for You—for who You are. You are my refuge, my shelter in the storm. You are my comforter, deliverer, my peace. You are all I need.*

*I bring the sacrifice of my praise to You and lay it on Your altar as an offering. Receive my offering, Lord, and return me to the joy of Your salvation. May my lips praise You and the meditations of my heart be a blessing to You, O my Lord. In Jesus's name, I pray. Amen.*

# Chapter Eight—Awaken the Dawn

> The candle in my heart was slowly burning into nothing, until He, like a dry match to a freezing man, rekindled my spirit.
> —A. Lee

Repair the altar.

Rekindle the flame.

And awaken the dawn.

Remnants of snow lay heavy on the stark branches of winter. A faint glow in the eastern sky spoke of the awakening dawn, pushing against the blanket of clouds covering the earth. Stillness. Silence. Just moments earlier, I had asked the Lord to quiet me with His love—to still my restless thoughts where anxiety lay. It was then I set my gaze toward the winter scene outside my window.

Then His peace unfurled and covered me with His wings.

I watched God's light bathe the earth with the newness of day—my thoughts could not escape the softness. *What are You saying to me, Lord? I sense Your voice trying to break through the clouds and darkness veiling my heart.* Taking another sip of coffee, I kept my eyes toward the eastern sky, my thoughts toward the Lord. The light outside my window grew warmer with each passing moment, yet the earth remained quiet. A holy hush settled as creation recognized the presence of God.

Tears pooled in the corners of my eyes as I too recognized His presence.

The Lord didn't come in like the roaring Lion of Judah that He is. Instead, He crossed over the mountain ridge at the breaking of the day like a Shepherd looking for His lost lamb—the one frightened and tangled in a web of overwhelming and suffocating darkness.

The glow of His glory reflected off the fallen snow, casting soft light through my window. As I sat in the light of His presence, tension released its grip on my shoulders. My mind no longer raced and wrestled with the taunts of the enemy. For my God was near. He had drawn near to my brokenness in the stillness of the morning light. He had quieted me with His love.

All through a holy hush of the awakening dawn.

I sat still and remembered He is God, and I longed for His embrace once more. Deep in my spirit, I heard His delicate whisper: *In quietness and confidence shall be your strength. Be quiet before Me. Still. Remain confident in My love for you. I will never leave you, nor forsake you. I will carry you when the road is long and the pain is great. I will lift you high into the heavenly places where no weapon formed against you will prosper. You are My child whom I adore. Be still. Be quiet. Like the glow of the awakening dawn, I am Your shield. I will light Your darkness and lead You on. But you must trust Me.*

In my darkest moments, these glimpses of intimacy with God would catch me by surprise. My heart was still very guarded, but I had decided to start taking the wall down brick by brick. My spirit gasped for breath, the tiny flame within longing to be rekindled like a dying ember in a fire. Often, I found my fingers skimming along the words of the psalms. I can imagine you do the same. Those of us crushed in spirit are drawn to David's honesty. There is something powerful about the strength of a spirit that has known the love and grace of God. Our minds may have checked out of holiness a long time ago, and our bodies may have become couch potatoes on Sunday mornings, but our spirits? Our spirits know the breath of God—*ruach*—that breathed life into us on the day of our salvation. Our spirits will fight for us until the end.

I found myself in Psalm 57 often:

> Be merciful to me, O God, be merciful to me!
> For my soul trusts in You;
> And in the shadow of Your wings, I will make my refuge,
> Until *these* calamities have passed by." (v. 1)

From the depth of my pain, I echoed these words to the Lord, "Be merciful, O God, for my soul trusts in You." I remember tears dripping as I fought to reconcile with the One whom my soul had loved.

We do not earn God's mercy. It is freely given. David was hiding in a cave being hunted like an animal by his enemies. God was his only hope. God is our only hope too. He knows our hearts before we utter a word. He knows our enemies of anger, betrayal, unforgiveness, bitterness, depression, and anxiety. He is the God who sees, who knows, and who cares. Charles Spurgeon reportedly wrote, "The sweetest prayers God ever heard are the groans and sighs of those who have no hope in anything but His love."

I love how David describes his enemies in verse four:

> My soul is among lions;
> I lie *among* the sons of men
> Who are set on fire,
> Whose teeth *are* spears and arrows,
> And their tongue a sharp sword.

That sounds about right, doesn't it? But let's follow along as David continues to strengthen his spirit in verse five:

> Be exalted, O God, above the heavens;
> *Let* Your glory *be* above all the earth.

In his anguish, David allowed his heart to remember the goodness of God. For a moment, he began to praise God. Perhaps he was reminding his soul to recognize God is worthy of all praise. Sometimes it only takes a moment, the first step, to begin our reconciliation with the Lord.

David waffled a little bit. Don't be surprised if you also waffle as you battle the enemy's clutches. Although David had just lifted his head to recognize God's presence in the difficult place with him, he quickly changed his focus back to his enemies in verse six:

> They have prepared a net for my steps;
> My soul is bowed down;
> They have dug a pit before me;
> Into the midst of it they *themselves* have fallen.
> Selah

Can you sense David's conflict of flesh and spirit? He is just like us. "There is therefore now no condemnation to those who are in Christ Jesus" (Romans 8:1). No condemnation. You have been nearly destroyed by unthinkable pain. God sees, knows, and cares. He understands your battle and is gently calling your name. In verse six, David is in danger of going back into the pit, but he doesn't let that happen. Let's not let it happen for us either. You are beginning to rekindle the flame within your heart.

In the wrestling match, David once again remembers who he is and who God is. He then speaks to his soul:

> My heart is steadfast, O God, my heart is steadfast;
> I will sing and give praise.

Awake my glory!
Awake, lute and harp!
I will awaken the dawn.

I will praise You, O LORD, among the peoples;
I will sing to You among the nations.
For Your mercy reaches unto the heavens,
And Your trust unto the clouds. (vv. 7–10)

Notice what happened when David declared the steadfastness of his heart. He began to sing. He began to praise. And his soul began to revive. The joy of the Lord became his strength. David worshipped God even in very difficult circumstances.

That made all the difference. He began to awaken the dawn of his soul.

Through the writings of Charles Spurgeon, I discovered Reverend August Tholuck, a German Protestant theologian in the early 1800s. I love his description of God's mercy and faithfulness as revealed in praise: "A hard and ungrateful heart beholds even in prosperity only isolated drops of divine grace; but a grateful one like David's, though chased by persecutors, and striking the harp in the gloom of a cave, looks upon the mercy and faithfulness of God as a mighty ocean, waving and heaving from the earth to the clouds, and from the clouds to the earth again."[1]

What a beautiful image! God's mercy and faithfulness are like a "mighty ocean, waving and heaving from the earth to the clouds, and from the clouds to the earth again." His mercy is great, flowing from the highest heavens to the lowest valleys for us. But if we do not intentionally awaken the dawn, His mercy, though there, will continue to be veiled in darkness. We have a choice.

But where do we start? As my fingertips move across the keyboard, I can sense your angst—you are at the jumping-off place, the place of reconciling with the One who loves you with everlasting love, the One who greatly disappointed and angered you. But look at you! Take my hand. We are going to do this thing together.

We know we have an enemy of the soul who takes full advantage of our crushing pain. But do you know who our worst enemy is most of the time? It's ourselves—our hearts. Jeremiah makes it clear:

> The heart *is* deceitful above all *things*,
> And desperately wicked;
> Who can know it?" (17:9)

What is our spiritual heart? It is the intersection of our thoughts, emotions, will, and moral compass. It is the very core of our being. Hearts can become calloused and keep us from turning to the Lord for healing.

Our heart is also the altar where the fire of God burns. Leviticus 6:12 teaches us, 'And the fire on the altar shall be kept burning on it; it shall not be put out. And the priest shall burn wood on it every morning and lay the burnt offering in order on it ... 'A perpetual fire shall burn on the altar; it shall never go out. Because of Jesus, we have been made "a holy priesthood, to offer up spiritual sacrifices acceptable to God through Jesus Christ" (1 Peter 2:5). We are the temple of the Holy Spirit. We cannot snuff out His flame, only dim it. He remains. However, the dimmer the light grows, the harder it is to see the evidence of God's presence in our lives. When deep calls to deep—when the depth of our pain calls out to the depth of God's love—His breath breathes on the spark left in our hearts, and slowly the embers begin to burn again.

But first, the altar of our hearts must be repaired so God's fire can fall again.

Is your heart broken? Has it simply become hardened or calloused? Is it eaten alive with unforgiveness that turned into bitterness and resentment? Have so many tears of sorrow fallen on the flame it is nearly quenched? I have good news. God is the God of the heart. Ezekiel 36:26 reads, "I will give you a new heart and put a new spirit within you; I will take the heart of stone out of your flesh and give you a heart of flesh."

Repairing the altar of our hearts takes work. It takes time. But primarily, it takes the first step. A decision. God will mend a broken heart if we give Him all the pieces. As we begin the work, let's pray together.

*Father, today is a day of decision for my friend. There is a huge conflict happening between her flesh and her spirit. Calm her restless thoughts and bring them captive to You so You might work. Call to my friend so she might look toward the sound of Your voice and behold her God. You know how hard it is to surrender our will to You, Lord. You know how hard it is to let go of the pain that is rightfully ours to own—pain that is justified and legit. But it is also destroying my friend and sucking the very life out of her.*

*Strengthen her, Lord. Give her the wings of eagles to rise above her difficult and broken places so she might recognize the chains and allow You to set her free. Make her brave. Make her determined to take her life back. Open the eyes of her heart that she might see You drawing near with mercy and longsuffering, awaiting her response and unclenched fist. Thank You, Lord, for working in the heart of my friend. Lead me as I lead her back into Your arms. Bless You, Lord. We give You praise.*

It feels good to talk with Him again, doesn't it? On my day of decision to allow God to begin softening my heart, He led me to Jeremiah 29. Most of us are familiar with Jeremiah 29:11, "For I know the thoughts that I think toward you, says the Lord, thoughts of peace and not of evil, to give you a future and a hope." I had been thinking about my future without my husband and a life marred by unthinkable betrayal. I was trying to reconcile my reality with God's promise. Then He showed me the *context* of this promise. Context can be eye-opening when applied.

To set the stage, consider my emotions at the time. I was right where you are now, paralyzed by emotions and unable to move forward, held in captivity. Before me flowed impossibility the likes of the Red Sea. On either side taunts and mockery of brokenness, dreams interrupted, and deep depression. Behind me surged the enemy's threats and rapid advance. I was stuck, held captive by unseen forces, principalities of darkness, and a heart growing harder by the day.

But didn't God promise me a hopeful future? Yes. He promised thoughts of peace and not of evil that would give me a future and hope. Yet I was still frozen, immobilized by captivity to my pain.

How many times have we quoted Jeremiah when life got hard and confusing? It is a go-to promise among Christian circles, and yes, it is a powerful truth that the Lord is sovereign and orchestrates every day of our lives. Even our days of captivity.

I turned to Jeremiah 29. The Lord asked me to put verse eleven in context—there was something I needed to understand. Chapter 29 of Jeremiah is a letter penned by Jeremiah to the children of Israel who, in 597 B.C., were carried away captive by King Nebuchadnezzar from Jerusalem to Babylon. Verse four reads, "Thus says the Lord of hosts, the God of Israel, to all who were carried away captive, whom I have caused to be carried away from Jerusalem to Babylon." God *caused* them to be carried away into captivity? Why? The Lord also instructed them to flourish in their captivity:

> Build houses and dwell in them; plant gardens and eat their fruit. Take wives and beget sons and daughters; and take wives for your sons and give your daughters to husbands, so that they may bear sons and daughters—that you may be increased there, and not diminished. And seek the peace of the city where I have caused you to be carried away captive, and pray to the LORD for it; for in its peace you will have peace. (vv. 5–7)

In its peace, you will have peace.

Flourish. The Lord calls us to *flourish* in our captivity—and to seek peace in that very place, to increase and not be diminished. How counterintuitive! But isn't this the very basis of trust? Determining to be at peace in the place—the season—we find ourselves in? Regardless? And then to determine to flourish there—to make a difference in the lives of others, magnify the Lord in all things, and bear fruit even if it must grow and thrive through the chain links wrapped around our very soul.

Yes, maybe that is what real trust looks like because just a few verses later comes that wonderful promise: "For I know the thoughts that I think toward you, says, the LORD, thoughts of peace and not of evil, to give you a future and a hope." But the promise does not stop there. The next verses read, "Then you will call upon Me and go and pray to Me, and I will listen to you. And you will seek Me and find Me when you search for Me with all your heart. I will be found by you, says the LORD, and I will bring you back from your captivity" (vv. 12–14).

He knows. He holds our tomorrows. And He loves us—deeply.

Perhaps God allows us to be carried into captivity so we fully learn to trust He is the One who is sovereign over our lives. He is the One who will bring us through to the other side restored and stronger because of the difficult, paralyzing place. I have learned God has an eternal perspective on all things. We are physical beings living in a physical world where everything is monumental to us. But to God, our lives are but a vapor. He is not constrained by time. His focus is helping us reach eternity with Him.

He is our exceedingly great reward. We learn the Lord Himself is in the pit of miry clay undergirding us, sustaining our lives while we wrestle and choke on our vomit of anger and disappointment. We learn *He* is the One who never changes, who remains steadfast regardless of how ugly our hearts become. Realization drops us to our knees, and we cry out, "Holy! Holy! Holy is the Lord!" ... and we find peace in the place of our captivity.

We find the Lord again.

It begins with humility.

Samuel Chadwick, considered to be one of the greatest preachers of English Methodism in the early 1900s, is believed to have said, "The prayer that prevails is not the work of lips and fingertips. It is the cry of a broken heart and the travail of a stricken soul." This prayer is authentic and raw, honest before the Lord. Confess your sin of unforgiveness, anger, or growing apathy. Sit quietly before Him and listen. Ask Him to shine His light into the darkened corners of your heart and acknowledge what He reveals to you. Own it, confess it, and rid your heart of its tendrils.

Repairing the altar must be intentional if we want to experience God's fire again. It requires the realization that the altar of our hearts is a place of daily communion with the Lord. It is where heaven meets earth—it is more than just a part of who we are. The altar has a depth of purpose. Seeing our hearts as the place of devotion and worship is a game changer. Restoration begins when we see the whole picture: repair the altar so we can rekindle the flame and rekindle the flame so we can awaken the dawn in our souls and have a fresh encounter with God.

When I first started trying to move forward, even though I still felt numb and calloused, I thought back on when I first met Jesus. Do you remember? Do you remember the wash of emotion as you experienced His love for the very first time? It's difficult to put into words, isn't it? And yet, the tangible evidence of His presence was all over you. Close your eyes. Sit there for a minute and remember. What were you doing when you first fell in love with Jesus? Do it again. Were you worshiping Him and singing His praise? Do it again. Did you open the Word of God with anticipation to see what He had for you each day? Do it again. Yes, do it again and again and again until the darkness begins to fade. Mother Teresa reportedly said, "When you have nothing left but God, you have more than enough to start over."

How do we rekindle the flame? And why? When we rekindle the flame of the Holy Spirit within us, His light penetrates our darkness, and we can recognize evidence of God's abiding presence. A realization occurs that the Lord never once abandoned us in our pain—we could not see Him because our circumstances consumed us. But before we can assuredly make an offering of that which crushed us, we must first stir the embers in our hearts. Remember? Restoration begins when we see the whole picture: repair the altar so we can rekindle the flame and rekindle the flame so we can awaken the dawn in our souls.

David and I heat our home with wood. Early on winter mornings, I open the stove doors to see glowing embers, red hot with hidden flames waiting to be rekindled. I toss some kindling on top and begin to blow on the embers. They ignite in response to my breath, and soon a flame spreads to the kindling as a fire is born. I cannot help but think of *Ruach Elohim*—the breath of God. His Spirit. His spoken word and how He responds to a willing heart that calls upon His name.

Think about it. When God spoke, His breath escaped His lips with every word, a billion stars were born, and the moon and the sun were hung in place. God spoke again—*ruach*—and the earth was formed, His breath traversing across every nook and cranny, every bit of vegetation and all creatures, bringing life. "And the Lord God formed man of the dust of the ground, and breathed into his nostrils the breath of life; and man became a living being" (Genesis 2:7).

Can you imagine the Lord molding Adam's body from the dust of the earth, cupping his face in His hands, and breathing life—His Spirit—into Adam's lungs? What a tender moment of a Father's love. *Ruach.*

And now, we are asking Him to breathe afresh on us and rekindle the flame of His Holy Spirit within us. Our heart is willing. Our hands are opened to receive from Him. If we listen, we will hear His still, delicate whisper deep within, speaking to our deepest needs, the breath of His Spirit making all things new.

He speaks to the fear, and it is gone.

He speaks to the chaos, failures, and confusion, and the breath of His Spirit demands that it go.

And when things go wrong, and we cannot catch our breath, our Father cups our face in His hands and breathes new life, new hope into our weary spirits. This rekindling thing sometimes takes time and surrender. It requires diligence that takes a stance and runs quickly to the Father when the pain resurfaces and triggers of pain sneak in the unguarded door seeking to separate us from the Lord once again. *Ruach Elohim*—the breath of God—responds to our call, stirs the embers, and reignites the flame within us.

I feel led to pray for you once again. I can sense the Holy Spirit is stirring in you and your emotions erupting. Let's pray and give it all to Him.

*Father, I can sense my sister's struggle, the tears of surrender forming in her beautiful eyes. Her heart is wounded, her spirit tattered and torn, and yet she is choosing You. At this moment, Lord ... she is choosing You. Would You unfold her fingers from the survivor's fist and hold her hand? Open her eyes to see her name engraved on the palm of Your hand and awaken her heart to love You once again. Breathe on her,* Elohim. *May Your breath blow upon the embers of her heart and light a fire within. Let her feel the warmth of Your presence, the reassurance of Your love, and the compassionate understanding You offer each of us in our struggles. Renew her, Lord. Set her free from the chains that have kept her bound and awaken her heart to worship You. Thank You, Lord. You are good ... so incredibly good. Heal my sister and set her free. Amen.*

We are learning to awaken the dawn in our souls. First, we must repair the altar of our heart that has been neglected. Afterward, God will breathe on us and send the fire. But what about the sacrifice? There must be a sacrifice to make an offering to the Lord. *We* are the sacrifice. The Apostle Paul exhorted the Christians in Rome, "I beseech you therefore, brethren, by the mercies of God, that you present your bodies a living sacrifice, holy, acceptable to God, which is your reasonable service" (Romans12:1). And that, my friend, means offering that which has created a barrier between us and the Lord. This brokenness has become our identity, stealing our lives, seeking always to snatch us from the Father's hand.

But nothing can separate us from His love. Nothing. "For I am persuaded that neither death nor life, nor angels nor principalities nor powers, nor things present nor things to come, nor height nor depth, nor any other created thing, shall be able to separate us from the love of God which is in Christ Jesus our Lord" (Romans 8:38–39). I know you know this. But in the depths of your despair, hasn't it felt as though God could not possibly love you? You could not even love yourself at times. Am I right? I know. I experienced that also. My heart had grown so ugly and calloused, especially toward the things of God. But then, through the power of His Holy Spirit, He began breaking through the darkness and calling me to Himself.

Could I let go? Could I lay my husband's betrayal upon the altar of God's great love? It would mean laying myself at the foot of the cross once again and remembering that I needed a Savior, a Redeemer. It would require me to admit that this thing—this pain that had gained immense value and importance to me—would need to be laid down *willingly* from my heart as an offering to the Lord.

As I became a living sacrifice, my heart would have to yield. That crushing pain of greatest importance—the first fruit of that life-altering tragedy in my life—would need to become my offering. If I were to become a living sacrifice, only the first fruit of my pain could be holy and acceptable to the Lord. Otherwise, I was just playing a game, deceiving myself and cheating the hand of God who was doing His best to restore me. He was doing His part, but I had to respond ... willingly.

Remember Exodus 27:20 gave instructions for lighting the golden lampstand in the tabernacle whose purpose was to illuminate the evidence of God's presence in the holy of holies: "And you shall command the children of Israel that they bring you pure oil of pressed olives for the light, to cause the lamp to burn continually." Pure oil was the first fruit of the olive, that which held the most value. Throughout Scripture, oil is symbolic of the Holy Spirit. This offering of the first fruit of the olive can easily be translated into the understanding that, when willingly brought before the Lord, our crushing pain will produce the oil of the Holy Spirit which reveals the evidence of God within our hearts.

The Hebrew word for first fruits is *bikkurim*. Translated, it means "the promise to come." Solomon, in his great wisdom, instructed the Israelites:

> Honor the LORD with your possessions,
> And with the firstfruits of all your increase;
> So your barns will be filled with plenty,
> And your vats will overflow with new wine.
> (Proverbs 3:9–10)

While trying to understand the principle of first fruits, I stumbled upon a writer and marketer, Jesse Wisnewski, who helps churches with digital tithing. These are his thoughts on the importance of giving God our first fruits: "They believed God was saying to them, 'If you bring Me your first fruits, I will bless all that comes afterward' ... Giving our first fruits means giving our best to God. It means sacrificing something that costs us something. It means putting God first, even before ourselves. Making a first fruit offering opens us up to allow God to work in our lives. When we approach God with open hands—rather than clenched fists—it makes it easier for Him to give us more to work with."[2]

Offering our emotional pain and brokenness as the first fruit of our hearts is an act of worship and sacrifice and an expression of thanksgiving, believing the shackles are finally coming off and our soul is awakening. How? Through the process. Our crushing pain releases the oil of the Holy Spirit which we have willingly decided to offer to the Lord to light the golden lampstand—the light of Christ within our hearts. This, in turn, will allow us to see the evidence that the Lord our God has remained with us throughout this horrific ordeal, and healing will begin.

I found something fascinating as I studied the first fruits. In the Old Testament, Moses gives instructions for the Feast of First Fruits (Leviticus 23:9–14 and Deuteronomy 26:1–11).

Deuteronomy, specifically, gives details. The Israelites were instructed by Moses that when they entered their Promised Land, possessed it, and then dwelled there, they were to take the first fruits of the earth and bring them to the place God chose to dwell. Next, the first fruits were to be given to the priest and placed before the altar of the Lord.

And then something remarkable got my attention. I am quoting Deuteronomy 26:5–10, but from the *Parashat Ki Tavo*, a section of the Torah used in Jewish liturgy during weekly readings. As you read the following passage from the Torah, I encourage you to view your journey (symbolically) through this passage. Apply it to your loss, trauma, and adversity that has no words. Read it expectantly, asking the Lord to quicken to you the deeper meaning and application to repairing your altar, rekindling the fire, and awakening the dawn of your soul.

> You shall proclaim before God your Lord: 'A wandering Aramean [Jacob] was my father. He went down to Egypt and sojourned there few in number, and there became a great, powerful and populous nation. The Egyptians dealt harshly with us and afflicted us, and put upon us difficult labor. We cried out to God the Lord of our ancestors, and God heard our voice, saw our affliction, our burden, and our distress. God took us out of Egypt with a strong hand, an outstretched arm, awesome acts, signs and wonders. He brought us to this place, and gave us this land, a land flowing with milk and honey. And now I have brought the first fruits of the earth that you have given me, God,' and you shall put them down before God your Lord and prostrate yourself before God your Lord.[3]

Before offering their first fruits, the people were to remember their journey with God and how their enemies afflicted them harshly. *Remember*. Remember what the enemy has done to you, what he has stolen from you. God did not cause your pain—the enemy of your soul did.

Recognize Satan's strategy to devour you and then, like the children of God, cry out to the Lord, your God. He hears you, He sees your affliction and distress, and He *will* deliver you with an outstretched arm and mighty acts of power. God wants to show Himself strong on your behalf. Notice that He brought His people out into a broad place and gave them their land of promise, just as He will do for you. Also, take note that in thanksgiving, the people brought the first fruits to Him—a sacrifice—and worshipped their God. They realized God hears. He sees. And He cares.

This is our model for deliverance—for gaining freedom from the shackles, repairing the altar, rekindling the fire, and awakening the dawn of our soul.

In addition, Jewish oral tradition teaches that before the Feast of First Fruits, the people proceeded to the temple singing a song of David recorded in the thirtieth psalm. It is a song of perseverance: "'I praise You, God, for You have raised me up and have not allowed my enemies to rejoice over me!' ... Its imagery speaks of being rescued from certain death, of being preserved by God from 'descending to the pit' and 'everlasting doom.' In it, David praises God, who has saved him from the clutches of his foes and has turned his mourning into rejoicing."[4]

*O Lord, You have raised me up and have not allowed my enemies to rejoice over me!* Hallelujah! Dear one, no longer will your enemies rejoice over you. Offering your pain as a first fruit will open the eyes of your heart to see Him once again. Though what you and I have gone through was devastating, is it any different than what the people of God have experienced throughout history? That statement does not negate your pain, nor mine, but it does put it into perspective. This is a fallen world where dreadful things happen to good people, but our God remains. He sees us and knows all about it. He draws near to us in our brokenness, whether we acknowledge Him or not, because His love for us is steadfast and longsuffering.

Psalm 30:5 reads, “Weeping may endure for a night, / but joy comes in the morning.” The Hebrew word for “joy” in this verse is *rinnah*. The *New Spirit-Filled Life Bible* notes, “*Rinnah* may best be illustrated by the testimony of the redeemed, returning to Zion from captivity. *Rinnah* is the word for both singing and joy.”[5]

Released from captivity, joy comes in the morning. Joy comes upon returning to Zion—to Jesus from captivity. Oh, my goodness! When we find peace in the place of our captivity, we will have peace. We will have joy once again.

How glorious is the moment when praise escapes our lips while tears course down our cheeks and the brilliance of sunrise heralds the dawning of a new day ... our new day. For our God is an awesome God, full of wonder, great in love. And though darkness has consumed us, He is there, waiting for the perfect moment to break through the inky jet of night and spill His brilliant light over all that pertains to us.

God sees. He knows and He cares.

A holy hush over the dew-laden earth awakens the dawn just as the reverent offering of our pain awakens the dawn of our souls. Are you ready to live again? Don’t be afraid. Every tear is precious to the Lord.

# Chapter Nine—Sacred Ashes

> When you stray from His presence, He longs for you to come back. He weeps that you are missing out on His love, protection, and provision. He throws His arms open, runs toward you, gathers you up, and welcomes you home.
> —Charles Stanley

Amber flames—cloud wisps in the morning sky—cast a golden hue upon the earth. Like the consuming fire of our God, the sky was ablaze with His glory. The darkness faded, overcome by the light.

My darkness has faded, replaced by the glory of His healing light. The Dayspring from on high, the Son of Righteousness, visited me and received my offering. David is now a permanent fixture in his recliner, but when I walk into the room, his eyes still twinkle. We make eye contact and speak with silent words. Knowing. Loving. Enduring. Though David's thoughts are random and difficult to follow at times, his spirit remains strong. I'm so thankful.

David prays for me often—he has even prayed for you as I worked on this manuscript. Although childlike most days, his prayers are where heaven meets earth. His words, chosen slowly but with intention, are like pouring the oil of the Holy Spirit upon my heart—the oil of most value, the oil born of crushing pain. In God's tender mercies, He shone

His light into the darkened corners of my heart, restoring the broken places, resurrecting where the death of dreams left its sting. I can now comfort you with the comfort I have received. I can offer you hope that has become a solid certainty of God's faithfulness to me.

The Lord longs to receive your offering and restore you to life once again. That place of darkness where pain has been unbearable, where nothing makes sense, and where the agony and shame of brokenness are more than you can bear is losing its grip on you. As you lay it on the altar found at the foot of the cross, its ugliness, lies, and destruction will lose its power. Our compassionate God will accept your offering of pain, His consuming fire engulfing the altar and creating beauty from its ashes. The light of His glory will dispel the darkness, and the bitterness will become a place of acceptance. Fear will transform into courage. Peace will rise through the amber flames. Oh, hear my heart, dear one! You will find, at last, it is well with your soul.

You will realize the ashes have become sacred, created by the glory of God's consuming fire. How else could beauty come from ashes? Only by the touch of His hand can such pain create beauty. But it is so. "Behold, I am the LORD, the God of all flesh. Is there anything too hard for Me?" (Jeremiah 32:27).

As I was writing, the Lord brought Abraham to mind, the story from Genesis where God called to Abraham and said, "Take now your son, your only son Isaac, whom you love, and go to the land of Moriah, and offer him there as a burnt offering on one of the mountains of which I shall tell you" (Genesis 22:2). Can you imagine the conflict within Abraham's heart? It had to be immense, perhaps like the conflict you may be feeling now. You know the Lord is speaking to you, asking you to trust Him enough with your pain to give it to Him, to lay it on His altar as an act of worship and obedience. But can you? Will you?

Abraham had to *willingly* prepare the altar for the burnt offering. God had instructed him to make his offering on Mount Moriah, a three-day journey from Beersheba. Upon arrival, Abraham gave the wood to Isaac to carry to the top of the mountain. He took the fire in his hand and a knife, and together they began their journey upward to the place God had told Abraham. Isaac questioned his father about the lamb to be sacrificed, and Abraham responded, "My son, God will provide for Himself the lamb for a burnt offering" (v. 8).

Can you envision this level of trust? You too are at a difficult place of obedience, perhaps with similar emotions as Abraham. He was preparing to offer that which was of greatest value to him—his son Isaac—while not understanding. Yet, he placed his hope in the One in whom he believed. Abraham did not know what the future held, nor did he understand why the Lord would ask him to do such a thing. But he surrendered his own will of holding on and chose trust instead.

This man of legacy and faith bound his son Isaac and laid him on the altar, upon the wood. Then Abraham "stretched out his hand and took the knife to slay his son. But the Angel of the Lord called to him from heaven and said, 'Abraham, Abraham!' So, he said, 'Here I am.' And He said, 'Do not lay your hand on the lad, or do anything to him; for now I know that you fear God since you have not withheld your son, your only son, from Me" (vv. 9–12).

I believe our lesson here is the recognition of God's presence with Abraham and Isaac in this difficult moment. He was with His faithful servant throughout the ordeal, just as He was with us ... and still is. The Lord searches our hearts and knows all our anxious thoughts. He also knows where there is rebellion and where there are wounds so deep recovery is unthinkable without His intervention. In this trial of the heart, Abraham learned his God is, in fact, *Jehovah-Jireh*, the Lord will provide. So, in many ways, not only is Abraham being put to the test but so is the Lord—Abraham's test of God's faithfulness.

*Jehovah-Jireh* revealed Himself to Abraham in the moment of obedient sacrifice. The profound assurance God would meet his needs—the ram caught in a thicket symbolizing Jesus as the substitution for our sin—is invaluable to us as believers, for He is our *Jehovah-Jireh*. All our heart lacks, He will provide. Trust makes the way. Obedience seals the deal. And the worship expressed in offering causes the Lord to reveal Himself to us in inexplicable ways of holy encounters, reassurance, and steadfast love.

For He is good, and His heart is turned toward His children.

The Lord wants, needs, and requires our hearts return to Him when we stray. Our covenant with Him cannot be broken, and the flame of the Holy Spirit within us cannot be extinguished ... but it most certainly can be dimmed by a hardened heart until we offer the crushing pain to Him. In the dimming, we cannot see the evidence that the Lord has been with us all along.

Jeremiah prayed this prayer of deliverance:

> Heal me, O LORD, and I shall be healed;
> Save me, and I shall be saved,
> For You *are* my praise. (Jeremiah 17:14)

This prayer came during a prophetic word to the Israelites about pending destruction if they did not repent of their foolish, rebellious ways. The people had trusted in man, their own deceptive hearts, and riches, but Jeremiah looked to the covenant God of Israel, for there he would find restoration—there, and there alone. The Hebrew word for "save" in this passage is *yashá* meaning "to rescue, defend, to free, preserve, deliver, and help ... The name of Jesus, *Yeshua*, is rooted in *yashá*. The original thought of *yashá* was 'to release,' 'to open wide.' Our Deliverer is the One who opened wide the gates of captivity, released, and rescued us, and continually defends and preserves us."[1]

I can't help but notice the word "captivity" once again. In Isaiah 61, Jesus explains why the Father sent Him:

> "He [the Father] has sent me to heal the brokenhearted,
> To proclaim liberty to the captives,
> And the opening of the prison to *those who* are bound ...
> To give them beauty for ashes,
> The oil of joy for mourning,
> The garment of praise for the spirit of heaviness;
> That they may be called trees of righteousness,
> The planting of the LORD, that He may be glorified." (vv. 1,3)

Oh, how I pray all these pieces are coming together for you. For too long, you have been held captive by that which almost destroyed you. The Lord is yearning to set you free so you might live once again. The willingness to offer your pain releases the oil of the Holy Spirit to fuel the light of Christ within you. The tiny spark becomes a flickering, bright flame illuminating the evidence of God in your life. With the light of Christ, the darkness flees. Hidden beneath the veil of darkness are the remembrances of God's faithfulness, the joy of your salvation, and the wonder and awe of being a child of the Living God. Now they are visible once again.

Yet the residual pain from your wound remains.

This is where the sacred ashes begin their ministry of comfort and restoration. God is a consuming fire. When He accepts our offering brought willingly before Him, His love consumes the pain, leaving behind nothing but ashes from which beauty will grow. In her blog post "God is a Consuming Fire!," Alexis Carucci wrote, "In the Old Testament, the fire of God consumed the offerings they placed upon the altar. In the New Testament, we are to put our lives on His altar as a living sacrifice saying not my will, but Your will be done (Romans 12:1). God's altar is holy because He is holy. As we repent, surrender, and obey Him, the Holy Spirit brings the fire. He purifies our hearts and consumes our sacrifice."[2] Ashes are left in the wake of His holy fire—ashes He promises to bring beauty from.

What do you suppose the beauty is? In my experience, the beauty that arose from my sacred ashes is the deep, personal knowledge of the Lord Himself. Deeper than ever before. Something happens when we decide to let go of what harmed us severely. We find rest. When our minds are troubled, our spirits are restless. But when we release the tormenting pain, rest begins and harmful thoughts cease. Recall for a moment George Matheson saying, "God's voice demands the silence of the soul. Only in the quiet of the spirit can we hear the garments of our God brushing by." Pause and consider that for a moment. This illustrates the Lord drawing near to our brokenness. In the tumult of our distress, we cannot hear Him. We cannot recognize His presence. But the action of laying that bundle of thorns on the altar is powerful! It breaks through the chains that have kept us bound. It quiets our soul, and we again join hands with the Father.

In my moment of surrender, the glory of the Lord's presence washed over me. Like a mighty rushing wind, He made Himself known—the motion of His love rippling His river within me. Stagnation departed. Peace resumed. Rest occurred. In the glory of His presence, my mind's eye could see my brokenness being consumed by God's holy fire and the ashes beginning to fall. I sifted them through my fingers and considered the magnitude of the moment. With my heart beating rapidly, I cried out to the Lord, *Help me, Father! Where do I go from here? You have excised my broken heart—I felt the release of its grip. But now I have ashes. What do I do with them? You promise to bring beauty, but how? Fill me up, Lord. Pour the fullness of Your Spirit into the empty place created in me. Awaken my heart to worship You, to seek You once again. Let me know You in fresh and new ways, deeper than I have ever known You before.*

I realized in my offering that the oil of the Holy Spirit had been released to fill the lamp of Christ within me. He reminded me of Isaiah 11:1–2:

> There shall come forth a Rod from the stem of Jesse,
> And a Branch shall grow out of his roots.
> The Spirit of the LORD shall rest upon Him,
> The Spirit of wisdom and understanding,
> The Spirit of counsel and might,
> The Spirit of knowledge and of the fear of the LORD.

Wisdom. Understanding. Counsel. Might. Knowledge. Reverence. My offering made it possible for me to fully grasp each of these ministries of the Holy Spirit. I had the opportunity to know the Lord with more depth than ever before.

And I was ready. I hope you are too.

God's holy fire burns away the dross—those things not of Him, those things cluttering our hearts, those things dimming the light of Christ within us. When our hearts are purified, we begin to see clearly. All He has ever been to us is now apparent once again. All about us are ashes—sacred ashes—of those things which brought us harm. They no longer have power over us.

Something I noticed as a direct result of offering my brokenness to the Lord was greater sensitivity to the things of the Spirit. Perhaps that was because of my renewed passion for the Lord calling me to devour His Word again and to worship Him in spirit and truth. The function of the Holy Spirit's oil directly correlates to rekindling the flame. Recall that the golden lampstand in the wilderness tabernacle had a central stem with three branches on either side. Scholars believe these branches are a direct reflection of the ministries of the Holy Spirit specified in Isaiah 11:2: wisdom and understanding, counsel and might, and knowledge and reverence. The Holy Spirit's ministries were flowing freely in me again, and my connection to the Lord was stronger than ever before. I could see and know with clarity. I now understand these six ministries are intricately connected *because* they stem from the Spirit of God. Through the Holy Spirit, I experienced rapid growth in each area as my wounds healed.

Because of my intense trial and process of offering, I became much more intimate with the Lord. My understanding of Him personally has become sealed and steadfast, my faith rooted deep in my knower where no one can take it away. The ashes have strengthened my roots, enabling me to hold fast when the storm winds blow.

As I consider my own heart in light of the golden lampstand, I have concluded that wisdom and understanding, counsel and might, and knowledge and reverence are connected to the greatest blessing of all I have received through this journey. Zechariah 4:6 reads, "'Not by might nor by power, but by My Spirit,' says the Lord of hosts." As I yielded to the Lord once again, I imagined the central stem of the lampstand (my heart) filled to the brim with the oil of the Spirit feeding every area of my life. I am acutely aware of His presence with me. My appreciation of His sovereignty is sure and uncompromised. I know *that I know* all I am and all I do is because of the God's Spirit within me. I have this full assurance now because I willingly offered my pain to the One who loves me.

And no one, nor anything, can ever take this knowledge from me.

I am forever changed.

The Apostle Paul makes mention of "attaining to all riches of the full assurance of understanding, to the knowledge of the mystery of God, both of the Father and of Christ, in whom are hidden all the treasures of wisdom and knowledge" (Colossians 2:2–3). That's it! Assurance. Understanding. Knowledge of the mystery of God—I found these treasures hidden in the wisdom and knowledge of Christ. What joy! What blessed assurance this brings.

Another beautiful fruit born of my ashes is the insight and wisdom I gained through the same letter to the church at Colosse. What I'm about to share has changed and strengthened me in unimaginable ways. I pray the blessings of joy that come from "aha" moments will also wash over you, and you will grasp this truth as you too are emerging from shattered faith. Colossians 2:9–10 reads, "For in Him dwells all the fullness of the Godhead bodily; and you are complete in Him, who is the head of all principality and power." In *Jesus* dwells all the fullness of the Godhead. The fullness of the Godhead is Father, Son, and Holy Spirit—the three in One. It occurred to me Jesus was God with skin on. He told His disciples that He and the Father were one, and if anyone saw Him, they were seeing the Father. Who is the Father? He is the Great I Am! I AM THAT I AM all you could ever need. At our moment of salvation, we traditionally say, "Jesus lives in my heart." And He does. But because Jesus lives in our hearts through salvation, the Great I AM is in residence there.

This new understanding of the Great I Am is significant to me because I realized the All-Sufficient God (*El Shaddai*) would meet my insufficiencies and make me whole. Whatever my need may be, the answer was dwelling within me—I AM THAT I AM. I suppose that seems like a simple truth, and yet I had never connected those specific dots before. Have you? The same Great I AM who delivered His people from the bondage of slavery to the Egyptians, who parted the Red Sea to swallow up their enemies, who fed them from His hand with manna from heaven, who loved them enough to give His only Son to die on the cross for their sins was setting me free ... The Great I AM dwells in me because of Jesus. And He dwells in you. Wow! This broadened my understanding of God's magnificence. It also intensified my understanding of how much He loves me. He would never abandon me but would be true to His Word.

> "Am I a God near at hand," says the LORD,
> "And not a God afar off?
> Can anyone hide himself in secret places,
> So I shall not see him?" says the LORD;
> "Do I not fill heaven and earth?" says the LORD."
> (Jeremiah 23:23–24)

God's holy fire burned away that which almost devoured me so that I could see, know, and understand His plans for me are good.

My friend, He is doing the same for you. Priscilla Shirer said, "The examples of Elijah, Hagar, Jacob, Moses and Gideon, Peter and Paul, and a whole bunch of others—has really encouraged me. Their examples remind me that even when my paths are hurtful, disappointing, earth-shattering, or unexplainable, those same paths can still put me in a prime position to experience God in a new way. To see Him from a new vantage point. To relate to Him and understand Him in a different, more mature, more dynamic way for the future."[3]

God will often lead us into times of solitude where we can regain our focus, where we learn invaluable lessons straight from His hand. Those times of stillness are vital in the life of a believer. But you and I placed ourselves into a self-imposed solitude. Am I right? I know I did. I withdrew into my own little darkened corner away from everything and everyone. I wasn't in the shadows thinking of Jesus—I was in the shadows wallowing in my brokenness allowing anger and resentment to fester. I was building a wall one brick at a time to keep the world and people and the Lord away. Like Elijah, I was done. Numb. Despondent ... until the Lord came to me. He found me in my difficult place and compassionately ministered to my heart's needs.

*What are you doing here, Nan?* He asked. *Who told you I abandoned You? Why has your countenance fallen and your heart hardened?* God will ask us questions He knows the answer to because He loves us enough to ask. He wants us to consider the condition of our hearts. Until we address the problem and assume responsibility for allowing anger, disappointment, and unmet expectations to build a wall between the Lord and ourselves, well ... we will continue to sit and sour. Miserably. Nothing will change.

But when we allow *Ruach Elohim*, the Breath of God, to come close enough to breathe on us, healing will begin. I promise.

On one cold, wintry day during my healing, the Lord taught me another lesson about His consuming fire. I opened the doors of our woodstove and stacked the kindling just so on the bed of newspaper and cardboard. Striking the match, I tossed it into the belly of the wood stove. After a couple minutes, the fire blazed enough to support larger logs. I laid some red oak and locust across the flaming kindling, closed the woodstove door a little bit to create a draft, and sat there soaking in the warmth on this frigid winter morning. And then to my amazement, the logs began to sing.

I had never heard this sound before. I'd heard hissing and, of course, crackling, but this was like a violin playing a single, mournful note. It was beautiful. I knew it must be moisture in one of the logs, but still ... it caused me to think.

The fire caused the log to sing.

The log sang because it had water inside.

As the heat released the water, a song was born.

Oh, my goodness. The fire caused the log to sing because it had water inside. The Lord reminded me at that moment that the deep river of God flowed swiftly within me. His holy fire could cause me to sing once more if I would yield to Him. When the fiery trials blaze all about us, lapping at our sanity, threatening to harm us, do we sing? Could we sing? Is it even possible to sing—to offer praise to the One who loves us? The answer, I believe, is yes!

Praise is available to us if we will allow it.

Perhaps praise and worship born of spirit and truth is the glory found in the ashes. This praise is not just a lip-synching, shallow song here and there, but a deep, holy, intimate, connecting-with-the-Lord kind of praise. The kind of praise He inhabits. The kind of praise that opens our eyes to see Him and awakens our hearts to know Him like never before.

Perhaps that is the song born of pain, a song created when the living water of the Lord is stirred and released by the flames of His holy fire. His fire makes the worship pure, holy, and acceptable to the Lord. His fire causes the praise to be a sweet aroma wafting to the heavens as its sacrifice reaches God's throne. Praise will set the captive free.

Freedom will surely come, but it can take time to be complete—God's time. We wait for the sunrise expectantly, for, without doubt, it will come. But it takes time. The ebony of night fades into ribbons of lavender swirling through a golden sky, and soon the sun crests the mountain ridge.

Like the darkness morphing into glorious light, so ashes will bring forth beauty.

In the last days of winter, I watch as snow peppers down outside my window, landing softly on the apple blossoms and bright green of freshly born leaves. The conundrum is obvious: Spring begins its unfolding while winter lingers. Spring will surely come in its explosion of color, but it takes time.

Answered prayer is like this. It requires waiting—waiting with expectant hope. When the needs of our hearts escape our lips and travel heavenward, the Lord hears. My heart remembers Psalm 37:5:

> Commit your way to the Lord,
> Trust also in Him,
> And He shall bring it to pass.

He will do it. But it takes time.

Consider the great oak born of an acorn. The oak tree was within the acorn, but it took a process. It took waiting, knowing that surely the great oak would grace the forest ... in God's perfect timing. It takes time.

What about the rose, branches stark and bare in the cold of winter? The bush is dreadfully bare. But then the warmth of spring's sunshine and showers of refreshing rain nurture this barren plant, and soon buds begin to form. The promised rose is maturing, waiting on its Creator's perfect timing, and growing in the process of waiting. Then one bright morning, dew glistens on the glorious crimson petals of the new blossom that had been within the stark, bare branch all along.

Sometimes God takes a long time to do something suddenly. Our prayers do not fall on deaf ears. Before the words have escaped our lips, the Lord is activating His response. But sometimes His response takes time to reach us. God's perfect timing and our willingness to offer the tormenting pain as a sacrifice brings about healing and transformative power—this sacrifice is of a magnitude only God would understand.

He's good like that. He knows this isn't easy. He knows your heart is wrenching in conflict, wrestling flesh with a persistent spirit. He hears your guttural cry for freedom. It's time to take His hand and allow Him to lead you on.

As sure as the sunrise is God's faithfulness to His children—His mercies are new every morning. His compassions never fail. What a glorious truth! I may have been crushed—you may have been crushed—but in the crushing of a child of God, the fragrance of Christ is released. The fragrance of Christ is beautiful, healing, and comforting. The fragrance of Christ testifies God's presence remains steadfast in our lives.

The sweet aroma shouts to the world that we belong to the Lord God—He is our portion, our inheritance. It announces to the enemy of our soul that what he meant for evil, God will use for good in our lives. When I remembered that—when I recalled His faithfulness—I found a grip on hope for a better tomorrow. That's when I emerged from shattered faith.

Now it's your turn.

May I pray for you once more?

*Father, Thank You for Your mercies that are new every morning, for Your faithfulness that reaches to the highest heavens and never fails. You are Wonderful, Counselor, Almighty God, the Everlasting Father, and the Prince of Peace ...* our *Prince of Peace. Thank You for Your peace that surpasses all understanding. Thank You for Your peace that transcends the highest walls built around the human heart.*

*My friend is taking down her wall, but it's hard ... so hard. Would You strengthen and encourage her? Would You lift her head to behold Your glory and allow her to see You face-to-face? Deep in her spirit, would You allow her to catch a glimpse of You drawing near?*

*She needs to be held for a while as she releases the unrelenting pain. It's excruciating. It's hard. But it's so necessary. I ask You to pour out Your blessings upon her obedient heart. Fill her to overflowing with Your joy once again. Let her know the sound of the chains breaking and clanging onto the floor as You set Your precious captive free.*

*You are* Jehovah-Rapha, *the Lord our Healer. I thank You for healing me, and I thank You for healing my sister. May Your healing balm of Gilead flow through her body, mind, and spirit erasing the damage done by her crushing pain. May her shoulders relax as the tension in her heart leaves. May the fountain of living water spring up within her and refresh her dry and thirsty spirit. I ask You dry her tears as only You can do.*

*You are good ... so good. Thank You for Your love and for Your healing touch. You are beyond wonderful. We offer You praise for You alone are worthy of all praise. You alone are God, and You alone satisfy the longing soul. Bless You, Lord. In Jesus's name I pray, amen.*

And amen.

The thought of my suffering and homelessness
    is bitter beyond words.
I will never forget this awful time,
    as I grieve over my loss.
Yet I still dare to hope
    when I remember this:

The faithful love of the LORD never ends!
    His mercies never cease.
Great is his faithfulness;
    his mercies begin afresh each morning.
I say to myself, "The LORD is my inheritance;
    therefore, I will hope in him!" (Lamentations 3:19–24 NLT)

# Afterword

On the following pages, I will help you process your journey of healing. I hope to assist you in placing your wounded heart, your crushing pain, and your distraught, damaging emotions on the altar of God's love. It's important to go beyond the emotional work by speaking it, writing it, and taking action to release it. Something powerful happens in the spiritual realm when we merge physical responses with spiritual desires.

In this space, you will find ten pages to process your lament, ten pages to process your offering, and ten pages to process your restoration and healing. Each page will have a truth from God's Word that will speak life to you, followed by a prayer prompt. Following the journaling section, I will offer some ideas for you to symbolically let go of what has held you captive.

I realize this step can feel awkward. I get it. But I also know that it will complete your healing process in many ways. Do you remember the day the Lord called your name to salvation? The act of coming to the altar, of telling someone—the act of physically responding to the miracle God had done in your heart—caused faith to arise. This is much the same.

To everything, there is a season,
A time for every purpose under heaven:
A time to be born,
And a time to die;
A time to plant,
And a time to pluck what is planted,
A time to kill,
And a time to heal;
A time to break down,
And a time to build up;
A time to weep,
And a time to laugh;
A time to mourn,
And a time to dance;
A time to cast away stones,
And a time to gather stones;
A time to embrace,
And a time to refrain from embracing;
A time to gain,
And a time to lose;
A time to keep,
And a time to throw away;
A time to tear,
And a time to sew;
A time to keep silence,
And a time to speak;
A time to love,
And a time to hate;
A time of war,
And a time of peace. (Ecclesiastes 3:1–8)

Dear one, now is your time to move forward and live again. You've got this.

I'm praying for you.

# Lament

The *Oxford Learner's Dictionaries* state that lament is "to feel or express great sadness or disappointment about someone or something."[1] I believe the act of lamenting is holy and acceptable to the Lord, an expression of deep trust in His love for us, an offering in its purest form.

Scripture provides many examples of those before us who wrestled with the reality of their suffering, released it to the Lord through raw, honest dialogue, and came out on the other side still declaring the goodness of God. King David is a prime example, as are Job and Jeremiah. A prayer of lament takes the struggling believer and leads them into a deepening relationship with the Lord. The result of expressing our anguish to Him is the return of His tender embrace, compassion, and reassurance of His unconditional love.

Aubrey Sampson offers a beautiful description for us: "Lament minds the gap between current hopelessness and coming hope. Lament anticipates new creation but also acknowledges the painful reality of now."[2] Isn't that beautiful? This thought expresses the very purpose behind these next few pages: bridging the gap between your hopelessness and opening your eyes to the coming hope of healing from our faithful God.

On the following pages, you will have the opportunity to pour out your heart before the Lord. I will give you a Scripture to meditate on and then a prayer prompt to get you started. Please don't hold back. Please don't think you need to sound pious and self-righteous. This is a time for honesty before the Lord, a release of the tentacles of deep, unrelenting pain that have held you captive.

I encourage you to find a quiet place where you can be alone with God—no interruptions, no pressing concerns, and devices turned off. Seek to be in God's presence, even though I know that may be hard until the anger and hurt let go. Ask Him to draw you close, to help you step out in faith beyond your pain so you can speak to Him honestly about it. And then ask the Holy Spirit to lead you in prayer that cuts to the quick of the problem, the root of the crushing pain, and to give you the courage to face this giant head-on.

The Lord is waiting with outstretched arms and a listening ear. He is permitting you to bring your rawest emotions to Him where He can bathe them in His grace, scoop you up in His arms, and begin the process of restoration. You have come through unparalleled difficulty—He knows this. You can count on Him to rescue you.

I'll close with this quote attributed to Charles Spurgeon: "Don't you know that day dawns after night, showers displace drought, and spring and summer follow winter? Then, have hope! Hope forever, for God will not fail you!"

*Selah*

## Day 1

### Lament

*Out of the depths I have cried to You, O Lord;*
*Lord, hear my voice!*
*Let Your ears be attentive*
*To the voice of my supplications.*

*If You, Lord, should mark iniquities,*
*O Lord, who could stand?*
*But* there *is forgiveness with You,*
*That You may be feared.*
*—Psalm 130:1–4*

Lord, in all sincerity I am crying out to You. From the depths of my heart, I am desperate for Your touch, Your love once again. Please help me! I don't understand why You ________________________________________

*Being completely honest with God is an expression of deepest trust, an acknowledgment of who He is. He is blessed by our honesty. —Nan*

## Day 2

### Lament

*HEAR my prayer, O Lord,*
*And let my cry come to You.*
*Do not hide Your face from me in the day of my trouble;*
*Incline Your ear to me;*
*In the day that I call, answer me speedily."*
*—Psalm 102:1–2*

Lord, I need to know that You are listening to me! Will You show me tangible evidence that You are with me, that You care about what I'm saying to You, what my heart is feeling? This is so hard because ____________________

*God is faithful to hear us when we call out to Him. The enemy of our soul mocks us, making us believe the Lord isn't listening. Stand fast to the promises of God—He hears. —Nan*

## Day 3

### Lament

*Have mercy on me, O Lord, for I am weak;*
*O Lord, heal me, for my bones are troubled.*
*My soul also is greatly troubled;*
*But You, O Lord—how long?*

*Return, O Lord, deliver me!*
*Oh, save me for Your mercies' sake!*
*—Psalm 6:2–4*

Lord, I can't do this any longer. I am weak with grief, tense with anger and disappointment ... in You! I don't want to be, but that's the way it is, Lord. Please help me. Please release me from ______________________________

*The Lord responds to authentic faith. He doesn't want pious platitudes. He wants us to trust Him with our hearts. —Nan*

## DAY 4

### Lament

*I am weary with my groaning;*
*All night I make my bed swim;*
*I drench my couch with my tears.*
*My eye wastes away because of grief;*
*It grows old because of all my enemies.*
*Depart from me, all you workers of iniquity;*
*For the LORD has heard the voice of my weeping.*
*The LORD has heard my supplication;*
*The LORD will receive my prayer.*
*Let all my enemies be ashamed and greatly troubled;*
*Let them turn back and be ashamed suddenly."*
*—Psalm 6:6–10*

Lord, I am so tired of feeling this way. I'm tired of being separated from You, yet here we are. I'm a shell of who I once was. I still want to blame You for ____________________

*Have faith! The Lord is listening. He is faithful and true, merciful, and kind. Your tears are precious to Him as He contemplates your struggle and longs to respond. —Nan*

## Day 5

### Lament

*See, O* L*ORD*, *that I* am *in distress;*
*My soul is troubled;*
*My heart is overturned within me,*
*For I have been very rebellious.*
*Outside the sword bereaves,*
*At home,* it is *like death.*

*They have heard that I sigh,*
With *no one to comfort me.*
*All my enemies have heard of my trouble;*
*They are glad that You have done it.*
*—Lamentations 1:20–21*

Lord, yes, I'm wallowing. There. I said it. Everyone is tired of my complaining, offended I keep pushing them away. But I need to do this my way, and everything I'm feeling is real. How do I________________________________

*God's name is* El Roi, *the God who sees you and knows all about it. —Nan*

## Day 6

### Lament

*I am feeble and severely broken;*
*I groan because of the turmoil of my heart.*
*LORD, all my desire* is *before You;*
*And my sighing is not hidden from You.*
*My heart pants, my strength fails me;*
*As for the light of my eyes, it also has gone from me.*
*—Psalm 38:8–10*

Lord, I'm tired. Weary. I'm struggling to find hope once again. I sense You trying to stir within me, but I'm not sure if____________________________________________

*Your sighing IS NOT hidden from the One who loves you with an everlasting love. His desire is for you to be whole once again, free to live, free to love, and free to worship Him. —Nan*

## Day 7

### Lament

*I will say to God my Rock,*
*"Why have You forgotten me?*
*Why do I go mourning because of the oppression of the enemy?"*
*As with a breaking of my bones,*
*My enemies reproach me,*
*While they say to me all day long,*
*"Where is your God?"*
*—Psalm 42:9–10*

Lord, the taunts of the enemy are relentless. Help me stand strong against him. I've listened to his lies for so long, it's hard to stop now. I find myself saying the same things to You: "Why ______________________________

*Our God is from everlasting to everlasting. He remains, just as He said. The light grows dim when our hearts are hardened, and we cannot see Him. But He is there in the shadows waiting. He will always wait for His child. —Nan*

## Day 8

### Lament

*My God, My God, why have You forsaken Me?*
Why are You *so far from helping Me,*
*And from the words of My groaning?*
*O, My God, I cry in the daytime, but You do not hear;*
*And in the night season, and am not silent.*
*—Psalm 22:1–2*

Lord, I made progress yesterday, but now I'm back to square one. My emotions are like a roller coaster. And my anger still boils when I least expect it. Why are You _____
_______________________________________________

*God's presence is not contingent upon our attitudes or emotions. His abiding presence is contingent upon who He is. He is faithful, and He promises to be with us always.*
*—Nan*

## Day 9

### Lament

*"How long, O* Lord*? Will You forget me forever?*
*How long will You hide Your face from me?*
*How long shall I take counsel in my soul,*
Having *sorrow in my heart daily?*
*How long will my enemy be exalted over me?*
*Consider* and *hear me, O* Lord *my God;*
*Enlighten my eyes,*
*Lest I sleep the* sleep of *death;*
*Lest my enemy say,*
*"I have prevailed against him";*
Lest *those who trouble me rejoice when I am moved.*
*—Psalm 13:1–4*

Lord, my eyes are beginning to open, and my heart beginning to soften ... a little. But the questions linger. I am still wrestling with________________________________

*The Lord would say, "You, child, are the apple of My eye, the joy of My heart. Your name is engraved on the palm of My hand. I will never forget My love for you." —Nan*

## Day 10

### Lament

*As the deer pants for the water brooks,*
*So pants my soul for You, O God.*
*My soul thirsts for God, for the living God.*
*When shall I come and appear before God?*
*My tears have been my food day and night,*
*While they continually say to me,*
*"Where* is *your God?"*
*When I remember these things,*
*I pour out my soul within me.*
*For I used to go with the multitude;*
*I went with them to the house of God,*
*With the voice of joy and praise,*
*With a multitude that kept a pilgrim feast.*
*—Psalm 42:1–4*

Lord, I miss You. Help me remember Your goodness. Help me bring my thoughts captive to You because they are filled with ugly, desperate memories. But You, Lord, are __

______________________________________________________

*With outstretched arms, the Lord is waiting for you. He will strengthen you; He will help you let go. He only needs a willing heart. —Nan*

## The Offering

C. S. Lewis once reportedly said, "Getting over a painful experience is much like crossing monkey bars. You have to let go at some point in order to move forward." My friend, this is the place you have come to, the offering—letting go of that which almost destroyed you. Almost. But you are stronger and more resilient than you know.

This step is hard but necessary. No one truly understands the pain you are feeling at this moment except you and the Lord. The struggle to let go is real. It's a pain too deep for words, and yet, our Father understands the groanings of your soul. He searches your heart and knows all your anxious thoughts.

I'm so proud of you. I know firsthand how hard this is. As you go through the process of laying your crushing pain at the feet of Jesus, the reality of His presence will begin to wash over you. Slowly at first. But the further you get into the letting-go phase, the more your spirit will join hands with Him once again. You will sense Him holding you while you weep, quieting you with His love. Chances are you will crumple into a tsunami of tears, but that's good. Tears are healthy, cleansing, and beautiful as an offering themselves. The Lord draws near to our brokenness, remember? Ask Him to open your eyes to see Him in your midst—to recognize His presence.

Your offering will release the oil of the Holy Spirit, and the flame within you will be rekindled, the light of Christ within you being set ablaze. You will experience the tormenting darkness shrinking as the glory of the Lord receives your offering and your soul begins to find peace once again.

I encourage you to begin unclenching your fist and releasing your pain to the Lord. Pour out your heart before Him, for He loves you and is waiting to set you free.

## Day 1

### The Offering

*The sacrifices of God are a broken spirit,*
*A broken and a contrite heart—*
*These, O God, You will not despise.*
*—Psalm 51:17*

Lord, I'm a mess—a broken mess. I long to be healed, to be put back together by Your mighty hand. I'm ready to let go, but this is a huge step for me. Will You help me? This crushing pain is too________________________________

*Giving your pain a name, be it anger, bitterness, or sorrow beyond description, is necessary for letting go. Sweet friend, what is it that has broken your heart and crushed your spirit? Call it by name. Out loud! —Nan*

### The Offering

*I cried out to You, O Lord:*
*I said, "You are my refuge,*
*My portion in the land of the living*
*Attend to my cry,*
*For I am brought very low;*
*Deliver me from my persecutors,*
*For they are stronger than I.*
*Bring my soul out of prison,*
*That I may praise Your name;*
*The righteous shall surround me,*
*For You shall deal bountifully with me."*
*—Psalm 142:5–7*

Lord, I can sense that You have heard my cry. Thank You. I am living in a pit of depression, tormented by the enemy all day long. I'm reaching out of the darkness, groping for Your ______________________________________________

*In her book* The Hiding Place, *Corrie ten Boom shares her sister Betsie's final words to her: "There is no pit so deep that He is not deeper still."*[3] *Betsie spoke these words as she lay dying in Ravensbruck, a concentration camp of the Holocaust. Beneath you, also, are the everlasting arms, capable and strong. He will catch you as you let go. I promise.*
*—Nan*

## Day 3

### The Offering

> The righteous *cry out, and the* Lord *hears,*
> *And delivers them out of all their troubles.*
> *The* Lord *is near to those who have a broken heart*
> *And saves such as have a contrite spirit.*
> *Many are the afflictions of the righteous,*
> *But the* Lord *delivers him out of them all.*
> *—Psalm 34:17–19*

Lord, hope is beginning to stir in my heart. I can feel it. I'm a little afraid to believe that I can be set free from this pain. Please give me the courage to [insert lines for responses________________________________________

*Dear one, you are still the righteousness of God in Christ Jesus. Nothing can ever separate you from His love—*we *are the ones that walk away from* Him. *His love is from everlasting to everlasting. He has heard your cry. Take hold of His hand, grip tight to that hope. It's yours to keep. —Nan*

## Day 4

### The Offering

*Therefore we also, since we are surrounded by so great a cloud of witnesses, let us lay aside every weight, and the sin which so easily ensnares us, and let us run with endurance the race that is set before us, looking unto Jesus, the author and finisher of our faith, who for the joy that was set before Him endured the cross, despising the shame, and has sat down at the right hand of the throne of God.*
*—Hebrews 12:1–2*

Lord, I know others have gone through this before me. But this is *my* pain! It's been a part of me for so long, I don't know how to let it go. It's heavy. I have allowed it to become a sin because I allowed it to separate me from You. I don't know how to fix my eyes on You. I don't know how to

____________________________________________________

*Take comfort in the knowledge that you are only human—many others have gone before you in their own pain and were able to come out victorious. Isn't that great news? Nothing is too hard for our God. He only needs a willing heart. —Nan*

## Day 5

### The Offering

*Create in me a clean heart, O God,*
*And renew a steadfast spirit within me.*
*Do not cast me away from Your presence,*
*And do not take Your Holy Spirit from me.*
*Restore to me the joy of Your salvation*
*And uphold me by Your generous Spirit.*
*—Psalm 51:10–12*

Lord, I don't pretend to know or understand Your ways, but You are clearly showing me that if I want my heart to heal, I must humble myself before You. I must ask You to create in me a clean heart. I know that is Your desire ... it's becoming my desire also. Lord, I confess to You that ____

______________________________________________

*Isn't it wonderful to know the Lord does not condemn His children? He gently leads us toward repentance, not for His sake, but for our own. His desire for you is that you be set free from your pain. Yielding your heart to Him is the first step. —Nan*

## Day 6

### The Offering

*"My soul, wait silently for God alone,*
*For my expectation is from Him.*
*He only is my rock and my salvation;*
*He is my defense;*
*I shall not be moved.*
*In God is my salvation and my glory;*
*The rock of my strength,*
*And my refuge, is in God.*
*Trust in Him at all times, you people;*
*Pour out your heart before Him;*
*God is a refuge for us.* Selah
*—Psalm 62:5–8*

Lord, my eyes are on You. I remember our fellowship of days long ago. I yearn for Your touch. I am trusting You with this devastation of my heart and asking that You give me the courage to thoroughly______________________________

*In the waiting, in the stillness, is where we encounter the Lord. That is where He stretches out His nail-scarred hands to receive our offering. —Nan*

## Day 7

### The Offering

*Then they cried out to the* Lord *in their trouble,*
And *He saved them out of their distresses.*
*He sent His word and healed them,*
*And delivered them from their destructions.*
*Oh, that men would give thanks to the* Lord *for His goodness,*
*And* for *His wonderful works to the children of men!*
*Let them sacrifice the sacrifices of thanksgiving,*
*And declare His works with rejoicing.*
*—Psalm 107:19–22*

Lord, I *will* offer You a sacrifice of praise, not for my sorrow but because of who You are. You are awakening my heart to love you again. You are healing me, and for that I am grateful. I trust You, but I don't trust myself to ________

______________________________________________

*The greatest way to honor the Lord is to offer Him a sacrifice of praise. It is a tremendous expression of trust, even when you don't understand—especially when you don't understand. I'm so proud of you for opening your heart once again. —Nan*

## Day 8

### The Offering

*I cry out to the Lord with my voice;*
*With my voice to the Lord I make my supplication.*
*I pour out my complaint before Him;*
*I declare before Him my trouble.*
*When my spirit was overwhelmed within me,*
*Then You knew my path.*
*—Psalm 142:1–3*

Lord, thank You for hearing the cries of my heart, and for surrounding me with Your love. I can hear Your songs of deliverance in the distance. I can hear the approach of Your angel army sent by Your hand to help me. Make me brave, make me ________________________________________

*Ask the Lord to open the eyes of your heart to see Him leaning in to hear your cries, to see Him coming to your side to strengthen and encourage you. When we seek Him with all our hearts, we will find Him. —Nan*

## Day 9

### The Offering

*I will love You, O Lord, my strength.*
*The Lord is my rock and my fortress and my deliverer;*
*My God, my strength, in whom I will trust;*
*My shield and the horn of my salvation, my stronghold.*
*I will call upon the Lord, who is worthy to be praised;*
*So shall I be saved from my enemies.*
*The pangs of death surrounded me,*
*And the floods of ungodliness made me afraid.*
*The sorrow of Sheol surrounded me;*
*The snares of death confronted me.*
*In my distress I called upon the Lord*
*And cried out to my God;*
*He heard my voice from His temple,*
*And my cry came before Him, even to His ears.*
*—Psalm 18:1–6*

Lord, it's been so long since I have told You I love You ... but I do. I always have. I was blinded by my brokenness and hardened by my perceived disappointment in You. But now I see. I see that You are ______________________________]

*The steadfast love of the Lord never ceases. His mercies are new every morning. Great is His faithfulness to you, my friend ... great is His faithfulness to you. He will restore, He will heal, and He will help you live again. —Nan*

## DAY 10

### The Offering

*And I said, 'This is my anguish;*
But I will remember *the years of the right hand of the Most High."*
*I will remember the works of the LORD;*
*Surely, I will remember Your wonders of old.*
*I will also meditate on all Your work,*
*And talk of Your deeds.*
*Your way, O God,* is *in the sanctuary;*
*Who* is *so great a God as our God?*
*You* are *the God who does wonders;*
*You have declared Your strength among the peoples.*
*You have with* Your *arm redeemed Your people,*
*The sons of Jacob and Joseph.* Selah"
*—Psalm 77:10–15*

Lord, I have sought You and I have found You. Finally, after all this time, I am ready to offer You that which almost destroyed me. I am placing it in Your hands. Seal this moment in my heart; help me ______________________

*Take a moment to give thanks to the Lord for His goodness. Think back on all the times He has been faithful to You and rest in those memories. They are powerful. They are true. And they display the glory of the Lord in Your life over all the years. —Nan*

## Restoration

Down the road, in a grove of chestnut trees, stands a home fully restored. Absolutely beautiful. But just a few years ago, it was a shell of its former self. Built in the late 1800s, this home once housed a thriving family. Church picnics were held on its grounds, children played hide and seek in the cornfield, and the sounds of laughter and love emanated from its walls.

But then disaster struck. Early in the 1970s, an ice storm took out the giant juniper in the front yard, crashing it through the roof of the old farmhouse. The family could not/would not/did not repair the damage, so the once-glorious home sat abandoned. Unattended. Broken and vulnerable to the changing weather and storms that crossed our mountains.

Recently, the dilapidated house was bought and restored. Old things were made new. Broken places made whole. It took time and thought. Perseverance and determination. It took the touch of a master carpenter's hand, but now the home is thriving with laughter and love within its walls again.

My friend, you, too, have endured the long and difficult process of restoration, but oh, how you will find it was worth it. You are no longer a victim—you are a victor, more than a conqueror. You made the decision and did the work.

You willingly offered your thoroughly crushing pain as a sacrifice to the One who loves you, and, in His mercy, He is bringing beauty from your ashes, laughter from your tears, and hope from your despair.

The Lord your God is giving you life anew. Healed. And restored.

Blessed be the name of the Lord!

**Day 1**

## Restoration

*Deep calls unto deep at the noise of Your waterfalls;*
*All Your waves and billows have gone over me.*
*The* L*ORD* *will command His lovingkindness in the daytime,*
*And in the night His song* shall be *with me—*
*A prayer to the God of my life.*
*—Psalm 42:7–8*

Lord, I called out to You from the depth of my pain, and You heard me. You responded from the depths of Your love—love so deep I cannot comprehend it—and You rescued me. Wash over me, Lord. Fill me to overflowing with ________

____________________________________________

*Take a moment to consider these words, "Deep calls unto deep ..." Picture yourself drowning in deep water, screaming for help. Out of heaven extends a strong hand reaching, grabbing ... rescuing you from your despair. That's the deep, deep love of our God. —Nan*

## Day 2

### Restoration

*I sought the Lord, and He heard me,*
*And delivered me from all my fears.*
*They looked to Him and were radiant,*
*And their faces were not ashamed.*
*This poor man cried out, and the Lord heard him,*
*And saved him out of all his troubles.*
*The angel of the Lord encamps all around those who fear Him,*
*And delivers them.*
*—Psalm 34:4–7*

Lord, thank You for not condemning me when I was angry and disappointed in You. Please forgive me. I had heard of Your faithfulness, even believed it, but now I see. Now I know that You are for me and not against me. Will You hold me and ________________________________

*Look up, dear one. There is no shame. God sees, He knows, and He cares. —Nan*

## Day 3

### Restoration

*Do not remember the former things,*
*Nor consider the things of old.*
*Behold, I will do a new thing,*
*Now it shall spring forth;*
*Shall you not know it?*
*I will even make a road in the wilderness*
*And rivers in the desert.*
*—Isaiah 43:18–19*

Lord, I don't know what tomorrow holds, but my eyes are on You. I ask that You bring my thoughts captive and help me cast down all imaginations so I may move forward with You. I choose You, Lord. Strengthen my faith to ______

______________________________________________

*Morning turns to day, then turns to night—every day. We know this to be true. We can depend on it. So is God's faithfulness to us. When He promises to do a new thing, He means it. Be expectant and full of hope. His goodness is coming up over the horizon. —Nan*

## Day 4

### Restoration

*Fear not, for I am with you.*
*Be not dismayed, for I am your God*
*I will strengthen you,*
*Yes, I will help you,*
*I will uphold you with My righteous right hand.*
*—Isaiah 41:10*

Lord, You are the Lion of Judah, mighty in power, fierce in protection of Your children. And You are with me. You always have been ... I am the one who shut You out and blamed You for my troubles. But I was wrong. Your love has never failed me. Open my eyes to ______________________

*Imagine the roar of the Lion of Judah as He walks beside you, daring your enemy to harm you. Why do we fear? He is a shield about us, a fierce protector. He is our God, and we are His people. Be brave and move forward in your quest for restoration. —Nan*

## Day 5

### Restoration

*Concerning this thing I pleaded with the Lord three times that it might depart from me.*

*And He said to me, "My grace is sufficient for you, for My strength is made perfect in weakness." Therefore most gladly I will rather boast in my infirmities, that the power of Christ may rest upon me.*

*Therefore I take pleasure in infirmities, in reproaches, in needs, in persecutions, in distresses, for Christ's sake. For when I am weak, then I am strong.*
*—2 Corinthians 12:8–10*

Lord, You are teaching me that Your grace is sufficient for me, but I must choose to reach out for it. That is a choice I want to make. I still don't find joy in my difficult places, but perhaps Your grace will______________________________

*I love that God's grace* is *sufficient. Not will be. Not might be. Not was. His grace* is *sufficient and available and is a game changer when we learn to receive it in our time of need. — Nan*

## Day 6

### Restoration

*Be sober, be vigilant; because your adversary the devil walks about like a roaring lion, seeking whom he may devour.*

*Resist him, steadfast in the faith, knowing that the same sufferings are experienced by your brotherhood in the world.*

*But may the God of all grace, who called us to His eternal glory by Christ Jesus, after you have suffered a while, perfect, establish, strengthen, and settle you. To Him be the glory and the dominion forever and ever. Amen!*
*—1 Peter 5:8–11*

Lord, I've had my fill of the devil, but I also know I can't be foolish. Keep me alert to his strategies to take me backward rather than continuing forward into Your place of restoration. I'm trusting You to ____________________

*We have been given authority over the enemy of our soul. At the mention of the name of Jesus, the enemy must flee. We are children of Almighty God, heirs to His kingdom. But we must choose to resist the evil one. We must choose to rebuke him in Jesus's name. Choose victory. —Nan*

## Day 7

### Restoration

*Trust in the* Lord *with all your heart,*
*And lean not on your own understanding;*
*In all your ways acknowledge Him,*
*And He shall direct your paths.*

*Do not be wise in your own eyes;*
*Fear the* Lord *and depart from evil.*
*It will be health to your flesh,*
*And strength to your bones.*
*—Proverbs 3:5–8*

Lord, Your love has drawn me back into Your arms where I remember how much I trust You. You have always been faithful to me. Thank You for Your forgiveness. Thank You for Your mercy that searches and knows my heart. Lead me, Lord. Show me how to move forward and how to ______ ______________________________________________]

*I have learned to trust in the sovereignty of God. He has an eternal perspective on all things—from the beginning until the end. Rest there, my friend. He does all things well in His perfect timing and in His perfect way. —Nan*

## DAY 8

### Restoration

*For this reason, I bow my knees to the Father of our Lord Jesus Christ,*

*from whom the whole family in heaven and earth is named,*

*that He would grant you, according to the riches of His glory, to be strengthened with might through His Spirit in the inner man,*

*that Christ may dwell in your hearts through faith; that you, being rooted and grounded in love,*

*may be able to comprehend with all the saints what is the width and length and depth and height—*

*to know the love of Christ which passes knowledge; that you may be filled with all the fullness of God.*
*—Ephesians 3:14–19*

Lord, my heart is beginning to fill with praise. Thank You! Because of my fiery trial, I have been rooted and grounded in Your love, and I have gained wisdom and knowledge. I have gained a new level of reverence for who You are. How can I thank You for ________________________

*Like Paul, I am praying for you to be strengthened in your inner man, and that your roots of faith will grow deep and strong in the knowledge of who He is. Who can measure the depths of His love? —Nan*

## Day 9

### Restoration

*But what things were gain to me, these I have counted loss for Christ.*

*But indeed I also count all things loss for the excellence of the knowledge of Christ Jesus my Lord, for whom I have suffered the loss of all things, and count them as rubbish, that I may gain Christ*

*and be found in Him ... that I may know Him and the power of His resurrection, and the fellowship of His sufferings, being conformed to His death ...*

*Not that I have already attained, or am already perfected; but I press on, that I may lay hold of that for which Christ Jesus has also laid hold of me.*

*Brethren, I do not count myself to have apprehended; but one thing I do, forgetting those things which are behind and reaching forward to those things which are ahead,*

*I press toward the goal for the prize of the upward call of God in Christ Jesus.*
*—Philippians 3:7–10, 12–14*

Lord, I, too, have lost so much to gain You and the true knowledge of who You are. Nothing compares to You. I need Your strength to press on, to forget those things which are behind and ____________________________________

*When we go through the fire and come out on the other side loving Jesus, we have found the pearl with the greatest price. The world cannot take Him away from us. We are sealed in the knowledge of His love, and nothing compares ... absolutely nothing. —Nan*

## Day 10

### Restoration

*Make a joyful shout to the* L*ORD, all you lands!*
*Serve the* L*ORD with gladness;*
*Come before His presence with singing.*
*Know that the* L*ORD, He* is *God;*
It is *He* who *has made us, and not we ourselves;*
*We* are *His people and the sheep of His pasture.*

*Enter into His gates with thanksgiving,*
*And into His courts with praise.*
*Be thankful to Him,* and *bless His name.*
*For the* L*ORD is good;*
*His mercy is everlasting,*
*And His truth* endures *to all generations.*
*—Psalm 100*

Lord, I feel Your embrace. I sense Your pleasure as You rejoice over me with singing. What an amazing God You are! I worship You. I give You praise, for You alone deserve my praise. I want to serve You with ____________________

*You have done the work. You have repaired the altar and rekindled the flame. Go now in the strength of the Lord. Remain humble before Him and fill your heart with praise, especially when you don't feel like it. —Nan*

# A Final Thought

The preacher spoke directly to me—his words flung from the pulpit straight to my heart: "Jeremiah wrote lamentations after his world as he had known it fell apart. But after his lament, Jeremiah reminded himself why he had hope—he *recalled* God's faithfulness." He remembered the mercies of God, His steadfast, covenant love.

When everything else was gone, God's mercies remained. His faithfulness continued.

You have discovered the same.

I applaud you. I pray you realize what you have accomplished. It's very difficult to let things go, to break chains, to bust through walls of pain. But you did it. Even on the hardest days, in the most painful moments, you did it.

I mentioned earlier that it is very important to apply a physical element to our spiritual decisions. Something about this completes the process, making a new life come alive. This is what I encourage you to do. Following are several suggestions of tangible things you can do to symbolize the offering of your pain.

- What caused you pain has now disintegrated into ashes—sacred ashes. Metaphorically, we can see them with our mind's eye. However, you may want to write out the details of your offering and set the script ablaze, creating actual ashes. I suggest you cast them into the wind while considering *Ruach*—the breath of God. Invite Him into this holy moment as the wind receives the ashes and scatters them about. You may want to go to a mountaintop to scatter them. You may be near an ocean, lake, or river where you can prayerfully release these special ashes to be carried away by the current. Allow them to sift through your fingers one last time as you let them go.

- Take the ashes, or choose a photo or item related to your pain and plant it beneath a rosebush. To me, the rose is extremely symbolic of the pain you and I have dealt with. When the petals of a rose are crushed, a beautiful fragrance is released ... *because* of the crushing. A rose isn't a rose without its thorns. Thorns march up the stem until they reach the lovely flower. Biblically, thorns represent sin, and yet they accompany the beautiful, fragrant rose. Can you see the parallel? Somewhere in the destruction of your heart lies sin, either of your own or most likely from someone or something else. How fitting it is to consider the rose as you take hold of your restoration, allowing your crushing to emit the sweet fragrance of Christ.
- Perhaps you could plant an acorn and tend to it over weeks, months, and years as it grows into a giant oak. Isaiah 61:3 tells us the Spirit of the Lord gives us "beauty for ashes, / the oil of joy for mourning, / the garment of praise for the spirit of heaviness." Why? "That they may be called trees of righteousness, / the planting of the LORD, that He may be glorified." What a fitting testament to your strength as you overcome your brokenness.

- Lastly, consider a river rock smoothed over time by the flow of the river softening its edges and polishing the coarseness of its surface. Maybe take several rocks and write on them specifically what you have endured. You can do this with one rock, or using several, each rock can identify individual emotions and consequences you had to overcome. As you sit by the river or creek, I want you to think, pray, and remember. When you are ready to let go, name them one by one, and cast them into the water as a symbol of surrender to the living water of Christ who sustains our life, washes us clean, and makes us whole again. If you write it in chalk, you can watch as the anger, depression, isolation, or bitterness evaporates and is no more.
- I encourage you to keep a record of how God is bringing beauty from your ashes. You could write your observations of the good things you are seeing in the margins of your Bible beside a favorite verse, or in a special journal so you can remember what the Lord has done. Being aware and looking for God's fingerprints as He brings you from brokenness to wholeness will keep you in tune with His redemptive work. Seeing your progress and remembering how God is faithful to you in the big things *as well as* the small things will keep you moving in the right direction. This will strengthen you and serve as a reminder on the days the enemy taunts you with his lies.

This journey together is coming to an end, but my prayers for you will continue. Remember that as sure as the sunrise is God's faithfulness to His children—His mercies are new every morning. His compassions never fail. What a glorious truth! I may have been crushed—you may have been crushed—but in the crushing of a child of God, the fragrance of Christ is released. The fragrance of Christ is beautiful, healing, and comforting.

The fragrance of Christ testifies to God's presence.

The sweet aroma shouts to the world that we belong to the Lord God—He is our portion, our inheritance. It announces to the enemy of our soul that what he meant for evil, God will use for good in our lives.

And when we remember that—when we recall His faithfulness—we keep a grip on hope for a better tomorrow.

*Selah*

# About the Author

God has called Nan Jones to help others recognize God in their difficult places. Through the written word and the spoken voice of her heart, she shares with you how to see beyond the veil and realize His abiding presence – through good and bad, through joy and sorrow, through peace and anguish. Nan served as a pastor's wife for thirty-one years. She is a popular Bible study teacher, speaker and writer quickly recognized for her compassion for hurting people. Her heart's desire is to help restore those who are broken to the Lord.

*The Perils of a Pastor's Wife*, Nan's first book, was a 2016 Selah finalist and Badge of Honor winner. Her award-winning blog, *Beyond the Veil*, helps her readers recognize God in their difficult places. She has been published in several anthologies, most recently with Guideposts, and served as a monthly contributor to Inspire a Fire for seven years. For three years, Nan had the honor of being a program producer for Hope Stream Radio, an internet radio broadcast out of Ontario, Canada with a global reach.

To connect with Nan, please visit her at NanJones.com. She is available as an inspirational speaker for conferences, retreats, workshops, or virtual events. No group is too small or large—Nan works within your budget. Contact information can be found at NanJones.com.

# Endnotes

## Introduction

1. Frances J. Roberts, *Come Away My Beloved* (Uhrichsville: Barbour Publishing, 2002), 34–35.

## Chapter One

1. "The Old Rugged Cross," George Bennard, 1912.
2. L. B. Cowman. Edited by Jim Reimann, *Streams in the Desert* (Grand Rapids: Zondervan, 1997), 344–345.

## Chapter Two

1. L. B. Cowman, *Streams in the Desert*, 113.

## Chapter Three

1. Beth Moore, *A Woman's Heart: God's Dwelling Place* (Nashville: LifeWay Press, 2007), 74.
2. David M. Levy, *The Tabernacle: Shadows of the Messiah* (Bellmawr: The Friends of Israel Gospel Ministry, Inc., 1993), 25.
3. David M. Levy, *The Tabernacle: Shadows of the Messiah*, 27.
4. Beth Moore, *A Woman's Heart: God's Dwelling Place*, 83.
5. David M. Levy, *The Tabernacle: Shadows of the Messiah*, 38.
6. David M. Levy, *The Tabernacle: Shadows of the Messiah*, 53.

7. Beth Moore, *A Woman's Heart: God's Dwelling Place*, 172.
8. L. B. Cowman, *Streams in the Desert*, 113.

**Chapter Four**

1. Jack W. Hayford, general editor, Roy Hayden, Old Testament editor, and Jonathan David Huntszinger with Gary Matsdorf, New Testament editors. *New Spirit-Filled Life Bible* (Nashville: Thomas Nelson Publishers, 2002), 1474.
2. Chris Fenner, "I Need Thee Every Hour," Hymnology Archive, March 27, 2019, https://www.hymnologyarchive.com/i-need-thee-every-hour.
3. L. B. Cowman, *Streams in the Desert*, 45–6.

**Chapter Five**

1. Joseph A. Cannon, "The Gospel in Words: Contrite," Deseret News, Aug. 14, 2008, deseret.com/2008/8/14/20379678/the-gospel-in-words-contrite.
2. L. B. Cowman, *Streams in the Desert*, 33–34.
3. 3. L. B. Cowman, *Streams in the Desert*, 269–270.

**Chapter 6**

1. L.B. Cowman, *Streams in the Desert*, 475.

**Chapter 7**

1. "The Complete History of the Serenity Prayer," Lighthouse Treatment Center, Aug. 3, 2017, https://lighthousetreatment.com/the-complete-history-of-the-serenity-prayer/.
2. *The New Strong's Exhaustive Concordance of the Bible* (Nashville: Thomas Nelson Publisher, 1990), 77.
3. Henri Nouwen, *A Cry for Mercy: Prayer from the Genesee* (New York: Doubleday, 1981), 17.
4. Jack W. Hayford, *New Spirit-Filled Life Bible*, 904.
5. Ibid.
6. Beth Moore, *A Woman's Heart: God's Dwelling Place* (Nashville: LifeWay Press, 2007), 103.

**Chapter 8**

1. Reverend Augustus F. Tholuck, *A Translation and Commentary of the Book of Psalms: For the Use of the Ministry and Laity of the Christian Church* (London: J. Nisbet & Co., 1856), 201.
2. Jesse Wisnewski, "A Short Guide to Understand First Fruits Offerings," Tithe.ly, Aug. 6, 2020, http://get.tithe.ly/blog/first-fruit.
3. Rav. Michael Hattin, "The Theme Behind Bikkurim: The Bringing of the First Fruits," Sept. 21, 2014, https://etzion.org.il/en/holidays/shavuot/theme-behind-bikkurim.
4. Ibid.
5. Jack W. Hayford, *New Spirit-Filled Life Bible*, 708.

**Chapter Nine**

1. Jack W. Hayford, *New Spirit-Filled Life Bible*, 984.
2. Alexis Carucci, "God is a Consuming Fire!," Living the Abundant Life, July 29, 2020, http://alexiscarucci.com/2020/07/29/god-is-a-consuming-fire/.
3. Priscilla Shirer, *Elijah* (Nashville: LifeWay Press, 2021), 202.

**Afterword—Lament**

1. "Lament," Oxford Learner's Dictionaries, accessed Oct. 5, 2022, https://www.oxfordlearnersdictionaries.com/us/definition/american_english/lament_1.
2. Aubrey Sampson, "Lament—What Does Lament Mean?" Unfolding Faith: Christian Living, Faith & Discipleship, accessed Oct. 5, 2022, https://www.tyndale.com/sites/unfoldingfaithblog/2019/01/22/lament-what-does-lament-mean/.
3. Ten Boom, Corrie, with Elizabeth and John Sherrill. *The Hiding Place* (Peabody, MA: Hendrickson Publishers, Inc., 2006), 240.

Made in the USA
Columbia, SC
13 August 2023

21527447R00109